The complete book of OFFICE MIS-PRACTICE

When faced with complete disaster TOTAL defiance is the __only__ recourse

The complete book of
OFFICE
MIS-PRACTICE

Paul Smith

Routledge & Kegan Paul
London, Boston, Melbourne and Henley

First published in 1984
Reprinted in 1985
by Routledge & Kegan Paul plc

14 Leicester Square, London WC2H 7PH, England
9 Park Street, Boston, Mass. 02108, USA
464 St Kilda Road, Melbourne,
Victoria 3004, Australia and
Broadway House, Newtown Road,
Henley-on-Thames, Oxon RG9 1EN, England

Set in Palatino
by Columns of Reading
and printed in Great Britain
by Hartnoll Print, Cornwall

Library of Congress Cataloging in Publication Data

Smith, Paul, 1947 Mar. 6-
The complete book of office mis-practice.

1. Office practice—Folklore.   2. Xerography—
Folklore.   3. Office practice—Anecdotes, facetiae,
satire, etc.   4. Urban folklore.   I. Title.
GR903.S64   1984   808.88'2   84-15920

British Library CIP data available

ISBN 0-7102-0434-5 [p]
ISBN 0-7102-0443-7 [c]

To
CATHY AND MIKE PRESTON

6

Contents

8

Preface

One Saturday afternoon I was shopping in the middle of Sheffield. While attempting to fight my way to the cash desk to pay for an electrical plug, I was suddenly confronted with the following proclamation taped to the side of the till:

ACHTUNG

Das Machine ist nicht fur Gerfingerpoken und Mitten-grabben. Ist easy schnappen der Springenwerk, blowenfusen und corkenpoppen mit spitxensparken. Ist nicht fur gewerken by das Dummkopfen. Das rubbernecken Sightseeren keepen hands in das pockets. Relaxen und watch das Blinkenlights.

Perhaps it was the heat of the afternoon but I remember mentally registering that it was odd that the till instructions were in German. It was only when I was leaving the shop that I realised the truth. I had found yet another example of a photocopied joke sheet – the product of a fast developing technology and one of the most prolific twentieth-century cultural traditions.

Somewhere in the majority of offices, and in many shops and works, you will find similar examples of photocopied sheets of jokes, cartoons, parodied letters, stories and songs. These are passed informally around the staff and, while they provide a great deal of entertainment, they also allow everyone, from the tea lady to the chairman's personal secretary, an opportunity to express just what they think of their everyday working life, their fellow workers and, of course, the boss. As the majority of us spend a great deal of our lives at work in offices, and the like, it is perhaps not surprising that an underground literature has developed which gives us an opportunity to comment on, and laugh at, our situation.

Like all cultural traditions, these photocopied sheets exhibit certain key features. First, the sheets do not exist as single items, as do works of art. Instead several copies of any one item will be, or have been, in circulation. Second, these copies will not all be identical but rather they will contain different versions of the same song, story or whatever. For instance, to date some 50 sheets containing versions of *A Letter from an Irishwoman to her Son* have been gathered (see page 131). However, these items are not all identical, instead they appear to represent at least six major and many more minor versions of this very popular spoof letter. In addition, it is not always the Irish that are singled out for this treatment. Some versions are presented as being written by Polish, Italian and even 'Newfie' mothers. A further aspect that cultural tradition and these sheets have in common is that both are essentially anonymous creations – although in reality they may have attributable authors or discoverable sources.

Each photocopied sheet, although originally a unique creation, now stands as part of a great tradition of 'unofficial' literature that has grown up since the Second World War alongside increased mechanisation in offices. The sheets fall into the category of 'unofficial' literature primarily because they are not part of any 'official' form of media or acknowledged institution for the exchange of ideas and information – such as the press or a publishing group. Instead the practice is for a few sheets to be produced on a small scale for 'free' circulation by individuals running off illegitimate copies on the office machine.

The popularity of these sheets appears to be in the way they allow us to express our views anonymously on our lot in life. You may, therefore, be reading and circulating a photocopied spoof memo that someone else has created but, at the same time, you are expressing your point of view by selecting sheets which you see as relevant to your own situation.

One of the major themes to be found in these photocopied sheets is a general dissatisfaction with the way business organisations and, for that matter, Government departments are run. This expression of dissatisfaction comes not from the outside but from the individuals who have to spend each day of their lives working within these organisations. Rather than being subdued or despondent with their lot they develop a quiet rebellion founded on caustic humour. Consequently, it is not surprising that photocopied sheets bearing such pointed philosophy as the following are passed around:

We the willing,
led by the unknowing
are doing the impossible
for the ungrateful.
We have done so much
for so long with so little,
we are now qualified to do
anything with nothing.

Alternatively, a large proportion of sheets not only ridicule the impersonal way people are often treated but also parody the bureaucratic machine itself. Although now somewhat dated, the *Company Policy on Streaking* (see page 28) is still one of my favourites – sending up bureaucracy at its best, or worst – depending on how you look at it.

Besides poking fun at bureaucracy many sheets share a common ideology with their humorous treatment of social and cultural values. Rather jaundiced views of sex and marriage are, for example, frequently aired.

However, not all photocopied joke sheets and cartoons are anti-establishment. A considerable quantity of the sheets currently in circulation could almost be thought of as anti-personal. For instance, the following statistical summary left on someone's desk, or arriving in their internal mail, provides a nice jocular way of saying – *Pull Your Finger Out!*

In view of the current financial crisis, the following figures may be of interest.

Population of the country	**54,000,000**
People aged 65 and over	**14,000,000**
Balance left to do the work	**40,000.000**
People aged 18 and under	**18,000,000**
Balance left to do the work	**22,000,000**
People working for the Government	**9,000,000**
Balance left to do the work	**13,000,000**
People in the armed forces	**2,300,000**
Balance left to do the work	**10,700,000**
Local Council and Government officials	**9,800,000**
Balance left to do the work	**900,000**
People who won't work	**888,000**
Balance left to do the work	**12,000**
People in Prison	**11,998**
Balance left to do the work	**2**

You and I, therefore, must work harder, especially you, as I am fed up running the place on my own.

The common feature amongst these sheets is, however, not so much the topics they explore or, for that matter, the way they tend to take an irreverent stand on practically every aspect of how we live and work. Instead, the common feature appears to be the way in which they achieve this end, in that they all contain a certain pointed humour and so tend to defuse tension and provide an opportunity to laugh at the source of our problem. For instance you may particularly dislike the Works Inspector but when you see him described as:

A survival of the Spanish Inquisition. Chief function is to weaken the operator's nerve, thus rendering him easy prey to the machine. This is accomplished by informing him that certain dimensions are undersize and, when adjusted, are then oversize by the same amount,

you feel less likely to hit him with a wrench and more likely to burst out laughing every time he appears.

In fact, because of their often humorous contents, these photocopies are frequently used in much the same way as jokes – specifically to entertain and amuse. I remember an incident some ten years ago when, late one evening, the bus on which I was travelling home was suddenly invaded by a crowd of young men out on a stag night. In the frolic that followed, one of the party suddenly drew a small clutch of well-thumbed papers from his wallet and proffered them to his mates. In no time at all these were being handed round and everyone was 'in on the joke'. The items that went round varied from sheets of one-line jokes to songs and cartoons. The intention was to raise a laugh and not necessarily make a point. However, irrespective of the goal, the technique is the same.

Although the technology now being used to generate these photocopied spoofs is comparatively recent, the notion of circulating 'unofficial' literature is far older. *The Spectator* for 10 May 1711 comments that political 'Accrosticks' were 'handed about the Town with great Secrecie and Applause' and also notes the existence of 'a little *Epigram* called the *Witches Prayer*, that fell into Verse when it was read either backward or forward, excepting only that it Cursed one way and Blessed the other'.

By the end of the eighteenth century broadside printers were producing items which, in terms of both format and content, demonstrate historical antecedents for the photocopy tradition. For

EXTRACT OF A

LETTER,

From an IRISH GENTLEWOMAN in

DUBLIN,

To her DAUGHTER in

LONDON.

From over against the Brick Wall Gate near the Common-Sewer, Dublin.

My Dear Child,

I Thought it my Duty incumbent upon me, to let you know that your only living Sister, *Carney Mac Frame*, has been violently ill of a fit of sickness, and is dead,—Therefore we have small or no great hopes of a recovery.— Your dear Mother did constantly pray for a long and speedy recovery.

I am sorry to acquaint you; that your God-Father *Patrick O' Conner*, is also dead,— His death was occasioned by eating a Calf's Head stuffed with Horse Beans and Gravy ! or, Gravy and Horse Beans stuffed with Calves Heads ; I don't know which. And notwithstanding the furgeons attended him three weeks, yet he died suddenly for want of help on the day of his death, on Sunday night last.—The great bulk of his estate comes to an only dead child in the family

I have made a present of your Sister's diamond ring to Mr *O Hara* the great small beer brewer, for thirty Guineas; and have taken the corner house that is burnt down to the ground on a repairing lease.

I have sent you Nine Shillings by the Chester carrier; the carriage of which comes only to a Guinea. Likewise, a Dublin Canary Bird which I have carefully put up in a rat trap, with some food in a snuff box, which will come free of all charges, only paying the Captain for the passage.

Pray send me news of the proceedings of the House of Commons next week, for we hear they have given us leave to import all our potatoes to England, which is great news indeed.

Write immediately and don't wait for the post. Direct for me at the *Bishop* and *Beef stak*, next door to the *Bible* and *Moon*, *Copper Alley, Dublin* for there I am now, but I shall remove to morrow into my new House. Dont send to me in a frank again, for the last Letter that came free, was charged thirteen pence.

Your Cousin in law, *Thady O' Dogharty*, is gone for a Light horseman among the Marines,

So no more at present from.

Your dutiful Mother.

Carney Cavenaugh Mac-Frame

P. S. I did not seal this letter to prevent its being broke open. Therefore send me word if it Miscarries; for the last letter that Miscarried came safe to hand

instance the broadsheet *Extract of a Letter, From an Irish Gentlewoman in Dublin . . .* , printed around 1795, provides an interesting parallel to *A Letter from an Irishwoman to her Son* (see page 131).

An intermediate stage, between the broadside tradition and the photocopied joke sheet, appeared in the late nineteenth and early twentieth century with the explosion of the postcard industry. A small percentage of the cards produced during this period carried, not pretty views of seaside resorts, but rather humorous verses and stories, such as *An Awkward Mistake*. Like the later photocopied sheets, the humour in these cards was based on parody and double entendre.

AN AWKWARD MISTAKE

A Young Man from Taunton, being engaged to a young lady and being desirous of buying her something for a birthday present and not being able to decide himself, went shopping with his sister. Entering a draper's shop she purchased a pair of knickers and he a pair of gloves for his lady love. A little error occured in sending the parcels off, with the result that the knickers were sent to the young lady instead of the gloves with the following letter:–

My dear Jessie,

I do hope you will accept this little token instead of a silly birthday card Oh! how I wish no other hands would touch them after you have put them on. I know dearest, that such a wish is in vain a thousand young men may touch them and other eyes than mine may see them on you. I bought the smallest size I could get and if they are too large let them rinkle down a bit.

Always wear them when we are together, as I want to see how they fit you. My sister says she has to clean hers every month as so many young men soil them with their hands, but you can clean them with benzine if you leave them on to dry.

I do hope dear that they are not too small and be careful, dear not to wet them and be sure to blow into them before you put them on

Yours with love,

PERCY.

However, both the broadside and postcard trades, while acknowledging the popularity of this type of humour, were of course operated as commercial enterprises. It was only when mechanical and electronic copying facilities were introduced into offices on a wide scale that we can say that sheets similar to those found today started to be produced for free circulation.

The first advance on this front came with the introduction of the typewriter. However, this would only allow the production of a few carbon copies. One early example of these sheets came to light a few years ago in the papers of a soldier who served in the First World War:

SOLDIERS' SUPERSTITIONS

It is considered very unlucky to be killed on a Friday.

It is unlucky for 13 to sit down to a meal when rations have been issued for only 7.

If the sun rises in the East, it is a sure sign that there will be stew for dinner.

To drop your rifle on foot of a second lieutenant is bad luck – for him.

To drop ditto on foot of sergeant major is bad luck – for you.

To hear lecture on glorious history of your Regiment indicates that you will shortly be going 'over the top'.

If a new officer, on taking over trench, announces that he has learned all about it at Cadet School, sign that he is about to get a surprise.

With the advent of various types of duplicator it became possible to produce more and more copies from a handwritten or typed 'master'. Certainly, up to 1960, the typewriter and duplicator were the most prevalent means of generating sheets of this type and occasionally items produced by these methods are still to be found in circulation today.

Photocopy machines became commercially available in 1949 and gradually, as their popularity increased, so did their official and unofficial applications. Over the last few years the advent of the coin-operated photocopier in libraries and shops has meant that this facility has been opened up to us all. Now, particularly within urban areas, the majority of us have some degree of access to what is, after all, the most technologically suitable piece of equipment for reproducing these sheets.

This does, however, have an interesting repercussion. Although nowadays more sheets than ever before are being passed round, the chances are that a higher proportion of them will be identical, as we no longer need to keep retyping and redrawing them. There is, therefore, less opportunity to amend, correct and elaborate existing sheets. Having said that, in some instances a steady elaboration has certainly taken place. For instance, the calculator spoof originally appeared without the memory function and clear facility, and was only available in a right-hand model. Gradually over the years inventive minds have upgraded the calculator into the sophisticated piece of technology we see today!

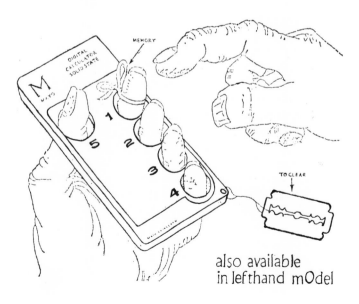

also available
in lefthand mOdel

Quite where the initial ideas come from for any specific item is not known. However, there is clearly a close and constant interrelationship between the photocopied joke sheet tradition, oral tradition, popular culture and all forms of mass media. Thus, material found in the form of photocopied sheets also occurs as commercially produced ephemera such as buttons, novelty cards and tee shirts. Similarly, 'literary' renditions of stories circulating as oral contemporary legends are also to be found in the photocopied tradition. In *The Book of Nasty Legends* I related, under the title of 'Not Your Lucky Night', the contemporary legend currently circulating regarding the boss who mistook his secretary's invitation to come home with her for a drink. The photocopy version runs as follows:

THE 49th BIRTHDAY

Two men sat at the club and one said, 'Say, how is that new secretary of yours?'
'Oh, I had to fire her.'
'How come?'
'Well, it all started a week ago on my 49th birthday. I was never so depressed. Well, I came down for breakfast and my wife never mentioned my birthday. I was sure the kids would remember, but not one word was said. As I say, I was most depressed but, when I arrived at the office, my secretary greeted me with Happy Birthday and I was glad someone remembered. At noon, she suggested that it was a beautiful day and that she would like to take me to lunch at a nice intimate little place in the country. Well, it was a nice place and we enjoyed our lunch and a couple of Martinis. On the way back she said it was too nice a day to return to the office and suggested that I go to her flat. Here she would give me another Martini. That also appealed to me and, after a drink and a cigarette, she asked to be excused while she went into the bedroom to change into something more comfortable. A few minutes later the bedroom door opened and out came my secretary, my wife and the two kids with a birthday cake, singing Happy Birthday, and there I sat with nothing on but my socks.'

A similar relationship exists between the photocopied joke sheets and other forms of oral tradition. The current vogue for ethnic jokes has found expression in both oral and printed forms, to the extent that any of the following jokes, taken from various photocopied sheets, might also crop up in conversation:

> Heard about the Irish Sea Scout – Went camping and his tent sank.

> Heard about the Italian Parachute – Opens on impact.

> Heard about the Irish Kamikazi Pilot – Writing his memoirs.

> Heard about the Polish Firing Squad – Formed a circle.

> Heard about the Italian Driver – Rolled forward in a hill start.

> Heard about the Kerry Nymphomaniac – borrowed a vibrator from Wimpey.

> Heard about the Irish Tap Dancer – Fell in the sink.

This interaction is not, however, limited to texts. Versions of photocopied posters, such as *The Job's not Finished until the Paper-Work's Done* (see page 69), have been found on commercially produced tee shirts. Likewise the notice, *As Soon as the Rush is Over* . . . (see page 59) frequently occurs as a novelty postcard. Given the existence of such a common core of traditional material, it is almost impossible to determine from where the material contained in these sheets was derived.

One important feature of the photocopy tradition is its international nature. For instance it is not unusual to find items, obviously derived from North America, circulating in the UK and Europe. Such sheets are immediately identifiable by their use of English, American spellings and so on. Irrespective of this anomaly, they are still acceptable and are quite happily passed around. Therefore, this collection of sheets, although in the main collected in the UK, represents versions which are currently circulating widely around Europe, North America, Australia, South Africa and probably any part of the world where photocopy machines are to be found. It would be wrong, however, to think of it as purely a phenomenon of the English-speaking world, for such sheets have also been found in German, French, Canadian French, Spanish and Swedish.

In preparing this volume I have not rewritten the sheets but rather reproduced them warts and all – the only concession being to supply the odd missing word or correct a totally misleading spelling. Any more would have been wrong for, irrespective of the state of the English, they all contain a certain raw immediate vitality. Besides, it would not be right for me, a mere mortal, to rewrite the great visionary wisdom handed down by these anonymous authors.

So remember, when things are getting on top of you and you need a little space in life, try pinning a copy of page 55 on your door. It is sure to work – one way or another.

Paul Smith
Yorkshire

To date several hundred photocopied joke sheets, cartoons and posters have been gathered. However, I am sure this is only just the tip of a vast iceberg and I would be grateful to receive from readers copies of any items not in this volume.

Paul Smith,
c/o Routledge & Kegan Paul plc.,
14 Leicester Square,
London WC2H 7PH.

Acknowledgments

By the time you have finished reading this volume you will be saying to yourself, 'I've seen sheets like those. There's one in the office at work.' For this very reason, my foremost acknowledgment must be to the thousands of people who type, draw, copy and pass on to friends and colleagues photocopies of these sheets. If it was not for all your efforts our working lives would be so very boring.

The items gathered together in this volume have been selected from a collection of sheets I have accumulated over the years. Besides my own contribution, the nucleus of this collection was founded on research by Georgina Boyes, Joe Goodwin, Cathy Preston and Mike Preston. To all four I owe an enormous debt. I must also thank the many friends who, over the years, have passed me examples of these sheets. In particular, thanks go to Ervin Beck, Jim Brennan, Geoff Dyer, Peter Eades, John Foreman, Derek Froome, John Hallam, Grey Hodnett, John Lake, Bill Quinton, Peter Millington, Ruth Richardson, Steve Roud, Doc Rowe, Ian Russell, Derek Schofield, Phil Smith, Andy Thomas, and John Widdowson.

In addition, I most gratefully acknowledge the pioneering work of a small but dedicated band of folklorists who, in spite of the conventions of their disciplines, have made us aware of the importance of this most active aspect of twentieth century tradition. In this respect I must acknowledge the work of Mac E. Barrick, Michael Bell, Georgina Boyes, Alan Dundes, Gary Alan Fine, William Ferris, Silvia Grider, Uli Kutter, Carl Pagter, Cathy Preston and Mike Preston.

Finally I must express my sincere thanks to Helen Hartnell, Derek Froome and Lisa Warner for their help in preparing this volume.

MEMORANDUM TO ALL STAFF

To All Employees
<hr />

We are asking that somewhere between starting and
quitting time and without infringing too much on the time
usually devoted to Lunch Period, Coffee Breaks, Rest
Periods, Story Telling, Ticket Selling, Vacation planning
and the Re-hashing of Yesterday's T.V. Shows, that each
employee endeavour to find some time that can be set
aside and be known as the WORK BREAK.

To some this may seem a radical innovation, but we
honestly believe that the idea has great possibilities. It
can conceivably be an aid to steady employment and it
might also be a means of assuring regular pay cheques.

While the adoption of the Work Break plan is not
compulsory, it is hoped that each employee will find
enough time to give the plan a fair trial.

The Management
<hr />

17th April, 1975

To Members of Staff,

TOILET FACILITIES - SURVEY

In connection with any possible move to centralised office accommodation, Departmental co-operation is requested in a survey to ascertain the requirements of toilet facilities with a view to instituting a centralised system.

The survey will commence on Monday 21st April, 1975 for a period of fourteen weeks.

Your co-operation is requested in the following way:-

1. Please record relevant details on the sheets provided in each water-closet compartment, each time you use these facilities.

2. Please record on a separate sheet the following details:-

    (a) date

    (b) length of visit

    (c) purpose of visit

    (d) distance travelled

    (e) face to face meetings/contact with five or fewer persons taking part (a separate sheet should be submitted for meetings with 6 or more persons taking part, indicating which one was on the chair).

Note: 1. Visits should be recorded as either "vacant" or "engaged" and any "engaged" visit should be reported to the switchboard immediately.

2. So that no confusion arises between a blank sheet due to absence from work and a blank sheet due to constipation, please indicate absence by returning sheet for the day concerned marked "absent".

Please forward your completed sheets to Wanlip by utilising the water borne communication system provided at the end of each visit.

Thank you for your co-operation. I trust you have not been inconvenienced.

Privy Time Utilization Report

Name _____

	Hrs.	Min	Sec	Tot.
1. Time spent in privy				

2. Sq. M. T-P used

mm.	cm	M	(Metric)

3. Sq. ft. Paper Towls used

ft.	In.	Yds.

4. Cubic ft. Water Involved in flush

ft.	In.	Yds.

5. CC. of Soap used to wash with

CC

6. Was Misson Successfull?

Y	N

7. Did You do a #1 ☐ or #2 ☐

8. If Misson was unsuccessfull
   fill in time on Idle Time Report.
      Your Cooperation will be
         appreciated.
         Thank You

COMPANY POLICY ON "STREAKING"

In view of the numerous inquiries Department Heads have had
regarding Company Policy on "streaking", the Management has adopted
the following:

1.   Streaking will be permitted as follows:

       Female employees will streak on odd days.
       Male employees on even days.
       On pay-day all employees may streak, subject to the following:

2.   Girls who have tattoos on the lower half of their bodies,
       such as "sock it to me" or "what you see is what you get",
       will not be permitted to streak. Also, men with tattoos of
       butterflies, roses or elves will streak with females.

3.   Junior executives may carry their brief cases while streaking,
       however, the usual rule applies - junior executives may
       never carry any business papers but may carry the usual,
       such as a box of Kleenex, lunch, wife's shopping list and
       Playboy magazines.

4.   Girls with a bust size larger than 36B must wear a bra while
       in the shop area or around moving machinery. Girls smaller
       than 36B should not try to impress people by wearing a bra.

5.   If you streak in any area where food is served you must
       wear two hair-nets. These will be available in the vending
       machines by the cafeteria.

6.   In the event that your physical make-up is such that your
       sex cannot be determined, such as flat chests for girls or
       long hair on boys, you must wear a tag stating "I am a boy"
       or "I am a girl". Tags will be attached on girls with hair
       pins or paper clips; on boys with rubber bands. Please
       return paper clips and rubber bands to the stationery
       supplies after you finish streaking.

7.   Girls may wear jewelry while streaking but in no event
       should they bend over to retrieve it should it fall. (Due
       to insurance regulations).

8.   No female beyond her seventh month of pregnancy, nor those
       wishing to become pregnant, may streak.

9.   No mixed streaking in dark hallways, broom closets or
       under desks.

AMSMT-YL   Points to Ponder

THRU AMSMT-YE   AMSMT-YL   22 Aug 68
         Mr. Clinto
      AMSMT-YZ
         Mr. Owen
      AMSMT-Y
         Col. Holston
TO   AMSMT-YT
         Mr. Lynch

In promulgating your esoteric cogitations or articulating

your superstitial sentimentalities and amicable philosophical

or psychological observations, beware of platitudiness. Let

your conversational communications possess a clarified

conciseness, a compacted comprehensibleness, coalescent

consistency and concentrated cogency. Eschew all

conglomeration of flatulent garrulity, jejune babblement and

asinine affectations. Let your extemporaneous descanting have

intelligibility and voracious vivacity without rodomontade

or thrasonical bombast, sedulously avoid all polysyllabic

profound vacuity. Shun double entendres and pestiferous

profanity whether recondite or apparent ....

.... IN OTHER WORDS ....

TALK PLAINLY, SENSIBLY AND TRUTHFULLY.

                         CHARLES A. THOMAN
                         Technical Liaison Staff
                         Missile Intelligence Directorate

Publication Division
Revision Section
Staple Group
% Larry Spoo

Dear Sirs:

Please be advised that one of our programmers
was caught actually removing a staple from a
Reference Manual revision. Investigation disclosed
that he had used a special 92 inch bolt cutter
and an M-3 hydraulic spike extractor.

I am aware that this is the only CDC staple
removed this year, but in order to prevent a
possible recurrence, the following is suggested:

Replace the present 32 gauge chrome-molybdenum
staples with the new 3 millimeter titanium-
impervium staples. These will need to be
inserted into the paper with a 500 ton steam
hammer, then bent over with a Mark II Laser
metal displacement unit.

With this new staple, mechanical and chemical
removal will be out of the question, and removal
by acetylene torch, which as we all know, was
almost successful in the Detroit incident last year,
will soon be found to be useless.

We will continue to advise you in regard to
in-house state of the art advancement in staple
extraction so that your counter measure group may
stay on top of it.

Yours very truly,

C. Blake
President
The "We Didn't Want To Revise The Damned
   Manuals Anyway" Club

To: Whom it may concern

From: R. Waltho

Date: 9th March, 1977

Company Cars - How to Recognise Them

Company cars have the following features rarely found in private cars:-

1.   They travel faster in all gears especially reverse.

2.   They accelerate at a phenomenal rate.

3.   They enjoy a much shorter braking distance.

4.   They have a much tighter turning circle.

5.   They take ramps at twice the speed of private cars.

6.   Battery, water, oil and tyre pressures are not required to be checked nearly so often.

7.   The floor is shaped just like an ash tray.

8.   They only burn the petrol with the highest green shield stamp rate.

9.   They do not require to be garaged at night.

10.   They can be driven for up to 100 miles with the oil light flashing.

11.   They need cleaning less often, especially inside.

12.   The suspension is reinforced to allow carriage of concrete slabs and other heavy building materials.

13.   They are adapted to allow reverse gear to be engaged whilst the car is still moving forward.

14.   The tyre walls are designed to allow bumping into and over stones.

15.   Unusual and alarming engine noises are easily eliminated by the adjustment of the fitted radio volume control.

16.   No security needed - they can be left with the key in the ignition.

APPLICATION TO BE ILL

This form must be submitted at least 21 days before the date on which you wish illness to commence.

Name

Clock Number

Department

Position Held

Nature of illness

Date on which you wish illness to commence

Applications to suffer from pregnancy must be submitted 12 months prior and be accompanied by **Form No. WS.36/24/9B.**

Consent of Husband/Wife

Have you ever applied to suffer from this illness before

If so, give date

Do you wish illness to be slight/severe/crippling/fatal

If illness is fatal do you wish this to be considered a permanent disability

Applicants wishing to suffer a fatal illness should indicate at the foot of this form whether they wish the Partners or Board of Directors to be represented at the funeral/cremation.

Do you wish to suffer this illness at Home/Hospital/Costa Brava/Kettering/ Torness/Kyle of Lochalsh

Do you wish this illness to be of a contagious nature

If so, indicate approximate number of people you wish to infect

Have you ever been refused permission to suffer from an illness

If so, give details

Do you wish your wife/husband to be informed of your illness if he/she contacts the company regarding your whereabouts

----

I, the undersigned, declare that to the best of my knowledge the answers given above are true and accurate.

Signed

Date

Applicants are reminded that all applications will be considered on merit and that more than three applications per annum will be considered excessive and not in the best interests of the Company. Under **no circumstances** will any employee be permitted to suffer more than **one** fatal illness.

MEMORANDUM TO EMPLOYEES   NATIONAL METRIC YEAR 1976

METRIC TIME

As doubtless you will have read in the National Press, from mid-night on 3rd April, 1976, the whole of Great Britain (except the Isle of Man) will be converting to Metric Time.

From that date, there will be 10 seconds to the minute, 10 minutes to the hour, 10 hours to the day and so on, delineated to the following table.

OLD TIME	NEW TIME
1 Second	1 Milliday
1 Minute	1 Centiday
1 Hour	1 Deciday (or Millimonth)
1 Day	1 Day
1 Week	1 Decaday
1 Month	1 Hectoday
1 Year	1 Kiloday

The fortnight will be withdrawn.

Obviously, from the part-time standpoint, due to the fact that one new hour represents only 5/12ths of an old day, employees might be expected to work longer hours, viz $3\frac{1}{2}$ decidays or millimonths per day. However, as this is inconvenient for administration and pay-roll purposes, it is intended that luncheon breaks will be shortened by $\frac{1}{2}$ a deciday, thus making a total daily working time of 3.542 hours, or 3 new hours + 5 centidays + 4 millidays.

It is not expected at this time that any compensation uplift will be made to salaries, except in the case of leap kilodays, where an adjustment will be built in at the end of the hectoday every 1.46 decamonths. Overtime will be paid to hectodaily roll employees for the time worked in excess of 5/6ths of a deciday, provided approval from local Social Security Office has been obtained beforehand.

Pension Schemes will not be affected by superkilodayuation will be adjusted accordingly.

A further bulletin will be issued closer to Deciday, but if these arrangements present difficulties or if you have any queries, please do not hesitate to contact your local Postmaster.

HOLIDAYS

Holidays will only be affected so far as the change to Metric Time is concerned and no one shall be worse off than previously. Thus, if any employee was entitled to 22 days (Old Time) he will now be entitled to 220 decadays, or one hectoday plus 20 decidays for every hectoday over and above 20 kilodays service since the 10th deciday of the third hectoday of 1954.

The term "A Month of Sundays" is not to be used on official documents. The correct term will be "A Hectoday of Decidays".

TO: STAFF

FROM: EX-EMPLOYEE

SUBJECT: OFFICE PARTY

When I came into the office this morning, I noticed a sort of general feeling of unfriendliness. Since several of you have openly called me a son-of-a-bitch to my face, I know I must have done something wrong at our office party last Friday. The office manager called me from the hospital and, as this is my last day, I'd like to take this way of apologising to all of you. I would prefer speaking to everyone personally but you all seem to go deaf and dumb whenever I try to talk to you.

First: To my dear and beloved boss, Mr. Simon, I am sorry for all the things I called you on Friday. I am very much aware that your father is not a baboon, nor is your mother a Chinese whore. Your wife is a delightful woman and my story of buying her for 50 cents in Tijuana was simply a figment of my imagination. Your children are undoubtedly yours, too. About the water cooler incident, well, you will never know how badly I felt about it and I hope they didn't hurt your head when they were trying to get the glass jar off.

To comely Miss Ashley, I express my deepest regret; in my own defence I must remind you that you seemed to enjoy our little escapade on the stairway as much as I did until the banister broke and we fell eight feet on to the second floor landing. In spite of the rupture you incurred when I landed on top of you, I am sure you will admit that when we landed it was one of the biggest thrills you have ever had.

Dave Jones, you old cuss, you've just got to forgive me for that little prank I played on you. If I had known you were jumpy I would never have done it. It could have been a lot worse if that fat lady hadn't been standing right under the window when you jumped through. She broke your fall a lot. People have been killed falling three storeys.

Mr. Gray, I regret telling that fireman that it was you who turned in the false alarm but, of course, I had no way of knowing that they would be such bad sports about it. Those fire hoses sure have a lot of pressure, don't they? And the water is so cold!

Bill Crane, you rate a special apology. My laughing when you forgot to put the seat down and got stuck in the toilet was bad enough, but my calling everyone else in to watch was unforgivable.

Bill Day, I know how you must feel about my opening the
door to the mop closet so suddenly. It must have startled you
and Miss Finch quite badly. When I think of how hard you
bumped your chin on the sink when you bent down to pull
up your pants, it makes me sick. We will have to get together
for dinner sometime when the dentist finishes your plate.

Miss Brown, the only excuse I can offer for stealing all of
your clothes and hiding them when I found you passed out in
the ladies' restroom is that I was drunk. Also, I want you to
know that I was very embarrassed when I couldn't remember
where I had hidden them and you had to go home in the old
sofa cover. Raising your falsies out on the flagpole was a bit
too much, I guess, but like I said, I was a bit drunk.

To the rest of you, I'm sorry. Setting Mrs. Bett's lace panties
on fire seemed a funny idea at the time, but it makes me sad
to hear that her husband is getting a divorce because of what
I did. Now that I have apologised to all of you, and I know I
will be forgiven, I've got a big surprise for you! Even though
I don't work here anymore, I'm going to do my best to get
back for the office picnic next Friday.

                    Your Friend and Ex-co-worker

RULES OF
THE OFFICE

RULES OF THE OFFICE

RULE 1

The Boss is always right

RULE 2

In the event of the Boss being wrong rule 1 applies.

RULES OF THIS OFFICE

1 This place has been designated as an '**off-ice**'. Here our employees may relax from the strenuous activities of home life.

2 Head of business shall be referred here-in as **EM-PLOY-ER**. NOT Fat-head, old-gum-shoe, old pinchgut, or other usual terms.

3 **IN CASE OF DEATH**, lie down. Name can then be dropped from payroll and committee will be appointed to collect fund for flowers and conduct lottery for deceased's former job.

4 Secretaries and file clerks must be given a handicap of 3 desk lengths before being chased through office. (At their own request, this rule shall not apply to female employees over 35.)

5 **IN CASE OF FIRE**
    (a) Awaken your sleeping fellow-employees SLOWLY to prevent nervous shock.
    (b) Leave by new steel stairway that management will erect immediately after this fire.
    (c) LEAVE like you do at 5 P.M.

6 **EMPLOYEES** shall feel free to make **SUGGESTIONS**. SUGGESTIONS cost NOTHING (and frankly, the ones that have been received lately are worth even less).

7 **WORK BREAK**. Starting Jan. 1 a new policy known as WORK BREAKS will be inaugurated. It is hoped that employees will try and fit this in their already busy schedule of coffee breaks, lunch hours, rest periods, vacations and days off.

OFFICE WORKING SCHEDULE

SECTION 1 - THE HOURS

8.30 to 10.30	Arrive at the Office
11.00 to 11.30	Morning Coffee Break
12.00 to 1.00	Lunch Break
2.00 to 4.00	Afternoon Tea Session
4.30 to 4.55	Prepare to Leave
4.55 exactly	Rapid Departure

WARNING: Any sign of intelligence or activity in this office should be regarded with the utmost suspicion.

SECTION 2 - THE TEN REGULATIONS

1. Thou shalt not do crosswords or read racing papers every morning.

2. Thou shalt not slip gin in the tea or take other spirited action - being at all times fairly sober.

3. Thou shalt not smoke or sing in the toilet.

4. Thou shalt try to keep awake during short periods allocated as "Work Breaks".

5. Thou shalt enter the office of the manager with great humility, knock on his door - enter therein - and kneel before his desk waiting for an audience.

6. Thou shalt not dress in any manner so as to arouse sexual lust in the office boys or tea ladies.

7. Thou shalt not steal thy neighbour's pens or pencils, nor his cigarettes, nor his cushion or pillow.

8. Thou shalt behave with decorum and dignity in the Office, not to train as a masseur during tea breaks.

9. Thou shalt laugh heartily at all jokes and puns - especially loud if made by a director or person in charge of wages and salaries.

10. Thou shalt most certainly keep thy wandering hands to thyselves.

****

FIRE INSTRUCTIONS

In case of fire, gather up all paperwork and run towards the flames.

SUGGESTIONS FOR 'GAINING TIME'

- Learn to say 'NO'.

- Control interruptions and improve the quality of your time.

- Delegate, with control, where possible.

- Be aware where your time goes. Keep a time-log for at least a week.

- Use the Pareto principle for allocating priorities to jobs.

- Stagger your working hours – e.g. lunch break.

- Work longer hours – a last resort.

1. Thou shalt not commit thyself lest thou maketh a mistake.

2. Thou shalt not become involved lest thou have to worketh.

3. Thou shalt not be consistant lest thine enemy perceive thy motives and thwart thee.

4. Thou shalt bump thy fellow worker lest he bump thee first.

5. Thou shalt be kind to thy fellow worker lest thou receiveth his wrath upon that time he becometh thy supervisor.

6. Thou shalt not ask whether thy work createth heat or light.

7. Thou shalt love and honor bureaucracy so that thy days shalt be lengthened.

8. Thou shalt not apply any efforts to thy work lest thy backlog be reduced and thy job abolished.

9. Thou shalt consistently introduceth new problem areas without defining the problem lest thy clear thinking illuminateth sacred confusion.

10. Thou shalt not permiteth management to knoweth of thy radical motives to improveth the system lest thou be brandeth a troublemaker.

MURPHY'S LAW

A set of maxims that seems to fill the gaps between all the laws, rules and regulations governing and explaining human behaviour.

- If anything can go wrong, it will.

- Nothing is ever as simple as it first seems.

- Everything you decide to do always costs more money than you estimated.

- Everything takes longer than you expect.

- If you improve, or tinker with something long enough, it will eventually break.

- If you try to please everybody, somebody is not going to like it.

- It is a fundamental law of nature that nothing ever quite works out.

- Whatever you want to do, you have to do something else first.

- It's easier to get into a thing than to get out of it.

- If you explain something so clearly that no one can misunderstand, someone will.

- Any time things seem to be going better, you've overlooked something.

- Nothing is impossible for a man who doesn't have to do it himself.

- Once a job is fouled up, anything done to improve it makes it worse.

- There's no such thing as a free lunch.

O'Toole's Rule: MURPHY WAS AN OPTIMIST.

RULES FOR DICTATORS

1. Never start work first thing in the morning. Typists much prefer a terrific rush in the late afternoon.

2. Please smoke while dictating. It assists pronunciation.

3. Do not face the typist whilst dictating. This would be too easy for her to hear.

4. Hours of dictation: during the lunch hour and at any time between 4.30 pm and 5.30 pm.

5. When dictating please parade up and down the room. Typists can understand what is said more distinctly.

6. Please call in the typist for dictation and then proceed to sort papers, look up old files, telephone and receive calls, etc.

7. Please lower the voice to a whisper when dictating names of people, places, etc. and, under no circumstance, spell them to the typists. Typists are sure to hit upon the right way of spelling them – they know the name of every person, firm and place in the world.

8. When typists do not hear a word and dictators are asked to repeat it, shout it as loudly as possible. The typists find this most gentlemanly. Alternatively, dictators should refuse to repeat them at all. The typists have second sight and it may come to them.

9. Whenever possible, dictators should endeavour to keep the typist late. Typists have no homes and are only too thankful to have somewhere to spend the evening.

10. Should a letter require a slight alteration after it is typed, score the word heavily through four times and write the correct word beside it – preferably in ink or heavy pencil – and always make sure the alteration is on the top copy.

11. Should a typist be too busy or too lazy to take down dictation, please write letters with a blunt pencil holding it in the left hand, whilst blind-folded. Incorrect spelling, balloons, arrows and other diagrams are very helpful to the typist.

12. Should work be required urgently (a most unusual occurrence) it aids the typist considerably if the dictator rushes in at intervals of 30 seconds to see if it is done.

13. If extra copies of a letter are required, this desire should be indicated after 'Yours faithfully' or over-leaf so as to ensure that it is the last thing that the typist will see when the letter is completed.

14. If a typist is making a tricky alteration requiring concentration and precision, always stand over her and breathe down her neck while she does it.

15. With regard to statements, do not on any account use lined paper. If figures are altered please write heavily over those previously inserted, the correct figure in each case being the illegible one underneath.

REPORT WRITING

RULES FOR WRITERS, EDITORIAL COMMITTEE AND PROOF READERS

1. Shun and avoid the employment or use of unnecessary, surplus, excess, extra words.

2. Make certain all sentences are complete. Where possible.

3. At all costs, avoid cliches and foreign phrases as you would the plague, ad libitum.

4. Take pane's to spel: and pucntuate corecttly"?

V 'bE CoNSistENT:

6. Don't approximate. Always be more or less precise.

7. Sedulously eschew the situative condition of obfuscatory hyperverbosity or prolixity.

8. Avoid pointless repetition, don't repeat yourself pointlessly.

9. Observe that, in all written expression, it is of the foremost importance if not, certainly not less than or at least not secondary to, the importance, of whenever possible trying, so that when, except where it cannot be avoided and/or in further necessary development it becomes imperative to omit, yet, you must remember without fail (for this must not be under-estimated) to be brief and clear. This is vital.

10. Always try to remexber the ~~extree~~ extreme importanse of being ~~aeur~~ accurate; neat and

CArrful.

PROCEDURE FOR MAKING ELECTRONIC MACHINES WORK

1. APPROACH THE AILING MACHINE IN A CONFIDENT MANNER. THIS WILL GIVE THE MACHINE THE (OFTEN MISTAKEN) IDEA THAT YOU KNOW SOMETHING. THIS WILL ALSO IMPRESS ANYONE WHO HAPPENS TO BE LOOKING AND IF THE MACHINE SHOULD SUDDENLY START TO WORK YOU WILL BE CREDITED WITH ITS REPAIR. IF THIS STEP FAILS TO WORK PROCEED TO STEP TWO

2. WAVE THE REFERENCE MANUAL AT THE MACHINE. THIS WILL MAKE THE MACHINE ASSUME THAT YOU ARE AT LEAST SOMEWHAT FAMILIAR WITH THE SOURCES OF KNOWLEDGE. SHOULD THIS STEP FAIL TO WORK PROCEED TO STEP THREE.

3. IN A FORCEFUL MANNER, RECITE OHM'S LAW TO THE MACHINE - (BEFORE TAKING THIS STEP, REFER TO SOME RELIABLE TEXTBOOK AND ASSURE YOUR KNOWLEDGE OF OHM'S LAW). THIS WILL PROVE TO THE MACHINE, BEYOND A SHADOW OF A DOUBT, THAT YOU DO KNOW SOMETHING. THIS IS A DRASTIC STEP AND SHOULD BE ATTEMPTED ONLY AFTER THE FIRST TWO HAVE BEEN TRIED.

4. JAR THE MACHINE SLIGHTLY. THIS MAY REQUIRE FROM A THREE FOOT TO A SIX FOOT DROP, PREFERABLY ON A CONCRETE FLOOR. HOWEVER, WE MUST BE VERY CAREFUL WITH THIS STEP BECAUSE, WHILE JARRING IS AN APPROVED METHOD OF REPAIRING A MACHINE, WE MUST NOT MARK THE FLOOR. AGAIN, THIS IS A DRASTIC STEP AND, SHOULD IT FAIL TO WORK, WE ARE FORCED TO PROCEED TO STEP FIVE

5. ADD AN INTEGRATED CIRCUIT. THIS WILL PROVE TO THE MACHINE THAT YOU ARE FAMILIAR WITH CIRCUIT DESIGN. ALSO, THIS STEP WILL GIVE THE MACHINE AN ADDED LOAD TO CARRY AND WILL THEREBY INCREASE YOUR ADVANTAGE. SHOULD THESE FIVE STEPS FAIL, WE MUST PROCEED TO THE MOST DRASTIC STEP OF ALL. THIS STEP IS SELDOM NEEDED AND MUST BE USED ONLY AS A FINAL RESORT.

THINK!!!!!!!!!!!!

The Simplified Modular Prose System

Honeywell, the American computer company, have devised this invaluable tool enabling those of us who can count up to ten to compose 40,000 well-balanced and impressive sentences. They call it SIMP for short.

To use it, think of a four-digit number. Any four-digit number will do – 1066 for example. Now read phrase 1 off Module A, phrase 0 off Module B, phrase 6 off Module C and phrase 6 off Module D, and you come up with:

> 'In particular, a primary inter-relationship between system and/or subsystem technologies is further compounded, when taking into account the evolution of specifications over a given time period.'

A sentence impressive enough for any report by an Eminent Authority to the Minister. To write the rest of the report, simply go on adding more and more four-digit numbers.

After you've mastered the basic techniques, you can realise the full potential of SIMP by arranging the modules in other orders: DACB and BACD. 'In these advanced configurations', warn Honeywell, 'some additional commas may be required'.

Please ignore the fact that the writing SIMP produces is totally meaningless. If you can put on a serious enough face when using the system, it's certain that everyone else will ignore the fact too.

SIMP

MODULE A	MODULE B	MODULE C	MODULE D
1. In particular,	1. a large portion of the interface coordination communication	1. must utilise and be functionally inter-woven with	1. the sophisticated hardware.
2. On the other hand,	2. a constant flow of effective information	2. maximises the probability of project success and minimises the cost and time required for	2. the anticipated fourth generation equipment.
3. However,	3. the characterisation of specific criteria	3. adds explicit performance limits to	3. the subsystem compatibility testing.
4. Similarly,	4. initiation of critical subsystem development	4. necessitates that urgent considera- tion be applied to	4. the structural design, based on system engineering concepts.
5. As a resultant impli- cation,	5. the fully integrated test programme	5. requires considerable systems analysis and trade-off studies to arrive at	5. the preliminary qualification limit.
6. In this regard,	6. the product configuration base- line	6. is further compounded when taking into account	6. the evolution of specifications over a given time period.
7. Based on integral sub-system considerations,	7. any associated supporting element	7. presents extremely interesting challenges to	7. the philosophy of commonality and standardisation.
8. For example,	8. the incorporation of additional mission constraints	8. recognises the importance of other systems and the necessity for	8. the greater fightworthiness concept.
9. Thus,	9. the independent functional principle	9. effects a significant implementa- tion of	9. any discrete configuration mode.
0. In respect to specific goals,	0. a primary inter-relationship between system and/or sub- system technologies	0. adds overriding performance constraints to	0. the total system rationale.

INTURPITASHUN
OF
SPECERFICASHUNS

THE PLANS and specerficashuns are to be taken tergerther. Aneything shown on the plans and not menshuned in the specerficashuns and not shown on the plans, is to be considdered as both shown and specerfied. And anything wanted by the ingineer or any of his friends, or by enybuddy else (except the contrakter) shall be considdered as shown, specerfied, implied, and required, and shall be pervided by the contrakter without no expense to nobuddy but hisself.

If the work has ben done without no expense to the contrakter, the work shall be taken down, dug up, or reworked and done agen until the expense is satisfak-tory to the ingineer.

Anything that is rite on the plans is to be considdered rite; enything that is wrong on the plans is to be discovered by the contrakter and shall be made rite without telling the ingineer or indercatin it in the bills.

Enything that is fergotten or left out of the plans or specerficashuns but which is necessary for the cunveenyence of the guy who is the owner shall be pervided without extry cost to enybuddy but the contrakter. The ingineer resurves the rite to change his mind about what is best.

IN TOUCH   Proud of your company's employer employee communication? Everyone knows what is going on? Think again, here is
a horrid warning!

Managing Director to Works Director

*Tomorrow morning there will be a total eclipse
of the sun at 9 o'clock. This is something
that we cannot see happen every day, so let
the work-force line up outside in their best
clothes to watch it. To mark the occasion of
this rare occurrence I will personally explain
it to them. If it is raining we shall not be
able to see it very well and in that case the
work-force should assemble in the canteen.*

Works Director to General Works Manager

*By order of the Managing Director there will be
a total eclipse of the sun at 9 o'clock tomorrow
morning. If it is raining we shall not be able
to see it very well on site, in our best clothes.
In that case the disappearance of the sun will be
followed through in the canteen. This is something
that we cannot see happen every day.*

General Works Manager to Works Manager

*By order of the Managing Director we shall follow
through in our best clothes the disappearance of
the sun in the canteen at 9 o'clock tomorrow
morning. The Managing Director will tell us
whether it is going to rain. This is something
which we cannot see happen every day.*

Works Manager to Foreman

If it is raining in the canteen tomorrow morning,
which is something that we cannot see happen every
day, our Managing Director in his best clothes
will disappear at 9 o'clock.

Foreman to Shop Floor

Tomorrow morning at 9 o'clock our Managing Director
will disappear. Its a pity that we cannot see this
happen every day.

17RSB/46

ONE FOR THE WALL

WOULD YOU BE VERY UPSET IF I ASKED YOU TO TAKE YOUR
SILLY-ASSED PROBLEM DOWN THE HALL?

LONESOME?

LIKE TO MEET NEW PEOPLE?
LIKE A CHANGE?
LIKE EXCITEMENT?
LIKE A NEW JOB?

JUST "SCREW UP" ONE MORE TIME

PLAN AHEAD

Be Like A Duck

ABOVE THE SURFACE LOOK CALM & UNRUFFLED...
BELOW THE SURFACE PADDLE LIKE HELL!!

AS SOON AS THE RUSH IS OVER, I'M GOING TO HAVE A NERVOUS BREAKDOWN.

I. WORKED FOR IT, I OWE IT TO MYSELF; AND NOBODY IS GOING TO DEPRIVE ME OF IT.

RUSH JOB CALENDAR

MIR	FRI	FRI	FRI	THU	WED	TUE
8	7	6	5	4	3	2
16	14	13	12	11	10	9
23	22	21	20	19	18	17
32	20	27	26	25	24	23
39	38	37	36	35	34	33

1   This is a special calendar which has been developed for handling rush jobs. All rush jobs are wanted yesterday. With this calendar a client can order his work on the 7th and have it delivered on the 3rd.

2   Everyone wants his job by Friday, so there are three Fridays in every week.

3   There are eight new days at the end of the month for those end-of-the-month jobs.

4   There is no 1st of the month so there can't be late delivery of end of the month jobs.

5   A "Blue Monday" or "Monday Morning Hangover" can't happen, as all Mondays have been eliminated.

6   There are no bothersome non-productive Saturdays or Sundays, no compensatory leave or overtime to worry about.

7   With no 15th, 30th or 31st, no "time off" is necessary for cashing salary cheques or paying bills – in fact, theres no salary cheque either.

8   "MIRDAY" A special day each week for performing miracles.

"Of course the order is wanted today!!! If it was wanted tomorrow it would have been ordered tomorrow!!!!!"

I'VE BEEN
  BEATEN, KICKED, LIED TO,
  CUSSED AT, SWINDLED,
  TAKEN ADVANTAGE OF AND
  LAUGHED AT,

BUT
  THE ONLY REASON I HANG
  AROUND THIS DAMNED
  PLACE IS TO SEE WHAT
  WILL HAPPEN NEXT !!!

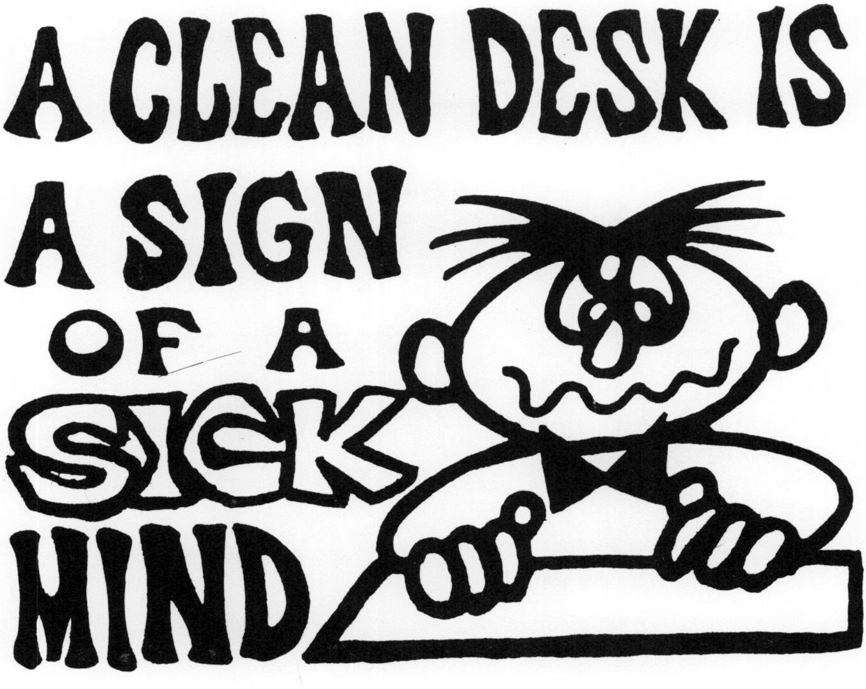
A CLEAN DESK IS
A SIGN
OF A
SICK
MIND

THE RUSH JOB

I belong to no age for men have always hurried.

I prod all human endeavour.

Men believe me necessary – but falsely.

I rush today because I was not planned yesterday.

I demand excessive energy and concentration.

I over-ride obstacles but at great expense.

My path is strewn with the evils of overtime, mistakes and disappointment.

Accuracy and quality give place to speed.

Ruthlessly I rush on.

I am the rush job!

"RESURRECTION"

People who believe,
that the Dead never,
come back to life,
should be here at
QUITTING TIME.

I'll be
right back—
Godot

If Today Doesn't
Get Better, Ill Have
To Have Sex

The Job's not finished
'till the paperwork's done!!

THIS IS TO CERTIFY

CERTIFICATE OF NON-ACHIEVEMENT

IS AWARDED TO

. . . .

who has distinguished himself by exceptional mediocre service during an indefinite but sustained period while serving in a position of no responsibility. During this period he was confronted by a variety of inconsequential challenges. His reaction to these trivial matters was to collapse completely. Unlike cooler, more level-headed contemporaries, he repeatedly crumbled under the slightest pressure. His flaccid standards could not fail to be met by even the most indolent individual, although he had difficulty in maintaining them himself. He has consistently displayed a total lack of knowledge of, or interest in, any facet of his position. During his tenure, because of his lackadaisical and indifferent approach, the position rapidly deteriorated to utter shambles. His inability to produce acceptable results under any circumstances characterised the insignificant effort he put forth. His selfish and uncooperative personality soon permeated his entire section to the extent that all with whom his section dealt were treated with hostility and contempt. His complete failure to accomplish a single given task stands as a tribute to those who wish to do away with the military establishment. His inebriated appearance, sloth, lack of ambition and odious traits of character, coupled with his 'to hell with it' attitude, have brought the utmost disgrace to his superiors and subordinates alike. His ineffectual substandard performance of duty is in keeping with the lowest tradition of humanity and reflects discredit upon himself, his country and society as a whole.

JAMES S. BYRD, MAJ.
Dept. G2

A ROUND TUIT

This is an indispensable item. It will help you
to become a much more efficient worker.
For years we have heard people say,
"I'll do it when I get round tuit". Now
that you have a round tuit of your
very own, many things that have
needed to be accomplished
will get done.

Certificate

FOR YOUR VERY OUTSTANDING
PERFORMANCE
YOU ARE AWARDED

"One Attaboy"

ONE THOUSAND "ATTABOYS" QUALIFIES YOU TO BE A LEADER OF MEN,
WORK OVERTIME WITH A SMILE, EXPLAIN ASSORTED PROBLEMS TO
MANAGEMENT, AND BE LOOKED UPON AS A LOCAL HERO, WITHOUT
A RAISE IN PAY,

NOTE: ONE "AWSHIT" WIPES THE BOARD CLEAN
AND YOU HAVE TO START ALL OVER AGAIN.

Mr. _____

REGRETS EXCEEDINGLY HIS DEPLORABLE CONDUCT WHILE A
GUEST AT YOUR PARTY

_____

AND HUMBLY CRAVES YOUR PARDON FOR THE BREACH OF
ETIQUETTE CHECKED BELOW:

☐ STRIKING HOST WITH BOTTLE.

☐ SPANKING FEMALE GUESTS.

☐ PICKING NOSE AT TABLE.

☐ THROWING FOOD.

☐ EXCESSIVE FURNITURE DESTRUCTION.

☐ COMPLETE LOSS OF EQUILIBRIUM.

☐ INDISCREET PETTING TACT.

☐ WEEPING.

☐ URINATING IN FISH BOWL.

☐ FAILURE TO BUTTON PANTS.

☐ LOCATING FEMALES NAVEL.

☐ UNFASTENING HOSTESS' GARTERS.

☐ LOOKING FOR HIDDEN MOLE.

☐ FREQUENT ABSENCE FROM PARTY.

☐ LOUD SINGING.

☐ STANDING ON RADIO.

☐ UNNECESSARY BELCHING.

☐ GUT RUMBLING.

☐ CHEWING HOSTESS' TITS.

☐ CARELESS VOMITING.

☐ SCRATCHING NUTS WITH SALAD FORK.

DIPLOMA

THIS IS TO CERTIFY THAT WE THE WILLING,
LED BY THE UNKNOWING ARE DOING THE
IMPOSSIBLE, FOR THE UNGRATEFUL.
WE HAVE DONE SO MUCH FOR SO LONG
WITH SO LITTLE, WE ARE NOW QUALIFIED
TO DO ANYTHING WITH 'NOTHING'

Interstellar Association of
TURTLES
Outershell Division

* * * * * * * * *

This is to certify

. . . .

is a member in good standing and will remain so as long as he continues to give the password when asked by a fellow Turtle.

As a member in good standing you can subscribe new TURTLES as follows:

I   We assume all prospective Turtles own a Jack Ass. This assumption is the reason for the password. This password must be given if you are ever asked by a fellow member, 'Are you a Turtle?' You MUST then reply 'You bet your sweet ass I am.' If you do not reply in full due to embarrassment or some other reason, you must forfeit a beverage of his choice. So always remember the password.

II   To become an official Turtle you must first solve the following riddles:

1.   What is it a man can do standing up, a woman sitting down and a dog on three legs? (Shake Hands)

2.   What is it that a cow has four of and a woman only two? (Legs)

3   What is a four letter word ending in K that means the same as intercourse? (Talk)

4.   What is it on a man that is round, hard and sticks so far out of his pyjamas you can hang a hat on it? (His Head)

III   You are now a member of the Turtle Club. Govern yourself accordingly and procure new members.

A TESTING TIME

Write a number of three digits on your paper. Be sure
that the difference between the first and last digit exceeds one.
Reverse the digits. Find the difference between the two numbers.
Reverse the digits of this difference. Add these two numbers.
Multiply by a million, subtract 966,685,433. Substitute these
letters for digits: Under every figure 1, write the letter L;
under every figure 2 write the letter O; under every figure 3
write the letter F; under every figure 4 write the letter I; under
every figure 5 write the letter R; under every figure 6, write
the letter P; under every figure 7, write the letter A. Read
the results backward.

DATE ....

NAME ....

TITLE ....

LOCATION ....

SITUATION ADAPTABILITY EVALUATION

FOR MANAGEMENT PERSONNEL

This test has been designed to evaluate reactions of management personnel to various situations. The situations are based on actual case studies from a well known educational institution and represent a cross section of test data collected to evaluate both reaction time to difficult situations as well as the soundness of each decision selected.

There are SIX multiple choice questions. Read each question thoroughly and place an "X" by the answer you feel is most correctly justified by the circumstances given. Be prepared to justify your decision.

You have FOUR minutes

1. You have prepared a proposal for the Regional Director of Purchasing for your largest customer. The success of this presentation will mean increasing your sales to his company by 2000. In the middle of your proposal the customer leans over to look at your report and spits into your coffee. You:

   a) Tell him you prefer your coffee black.

   b) Ask to have him checked for any communicable diseases.

   c) Take a leak in his "out" basket.

2. You are having lunch with a prospective customer talking about what could be your biggest sale of the year. During the conversation a blonde walks into the restaurant and she is so stunning you draw your companion's attention to her and give a vivid description of what you would do if you had her alone in your motel. She walks over to the table and introduces herself as your client's daughter. Your next move is to:

   a) Ask for her hand in marriage.

   b) Pretend you've forgotten how to speak English.

   c) Repeat the conversation to the daughter and just hope for the best.

3. You are making a sales presentation to a group of corporate executives in the plushest office you've ever seen. The hot chilli con carne and egg salad sandwich you had for lunch react creating a severe pressure. Your sphincter loses its control and you break wind in the most convincing manner causing three water tumblers to shatter and a secretary to pass out. What you should do next is:

a) Offer to come back next week when the smell has gone away.

b) Point out their chief executive and accuse him of the offense.

c) Challenge anyone in the room to do better.

4. You are at a business lunch when you are suddenly overcome with an uncontrollable desire to pick your nose. Remembering this is definitely a NO-NO, you:

a) Pretend to wave to someone across the room and with one fluid motion, bury your forefinger in your nostril right up to the fourth joint.

b) Get everyone drunk and organise a nose picking contest with a prize for the one who makes his nose bleed first.

c) Drop your napkin on the floor and when you bend over to pick it up, blow your nose on your sock.

5. You've just spent the evening with a supplier who invited you to an all night boiler-maker drinking party. You get home just in time to go to work. You stagger to the men's room and spend the next half hour vomiting. As you're washing up at the sink, the Sales Training Director walks up and blows his cigar in your face and asks you to join him for drinks after work. You:

a) Look him straight in the eye and launch one last convulsive torrent at the front of his Savile Row suit.

b) Nail him in the crotch, banking on the fact that he'll never recognise your green face.

c) Grasp his hand and pump it until he pees in his pants.

6. You're on your way to see your best account when your zipper breaks and you discover that you forgot to put on your underpants that morning. You decide to:

a) Call on the customer's secretary instead.

b) Explain you were just trolling for queers.

c) Buy a baggy raincoat and head for the school playground.

FINAL EXAMINATION

INSTRUCTIONS: Read each question carefully. Answer all questions.
Time Limit: 4 hours. Begin immediately.

1. **HISTORY**
Describe the history of the papacy from its origins to the present, concentrating especially but not exclusively on its social, political, economic, religious, and philosophical impact on Europe, Asia, America, and Africa. Be brief, concise, and specific.

2. **MEDICINE**
You have been provided with a razor blade, a piece of gauze, and a bottle of scotch. Remove your appendix. Do not suture until your work has been inspected. You have fifteen minutes.

3. **PUBLIC SPEAKING**
2500 riot-crazed aborigines are storming the classroom. Calm them. You may use any ancient language except Latin or Greek.

4. **BIOLOGY**
Create Life. Estimate the differences in subsequent human culture if this form of life had developed 500 million years earlier, with special attention to its probable effect on the English parliamentary system. Prove your thesis.

5. **MUSIC**
Write a piano concerto. Orchestrate and perform it with flute and drum. You will find a piano under your seat.

6. **PSYCHOLOGY**
Based on your knowledge of their works, evaluate the emotional stability, degree of adjustment, and repressed frustrations of each of the following: Alexander of Aphrodisias, Rameses II, Gregory of Nices, and Hammurabi. Support your thesis with quotations from each man's work, making appropriate references. It is not necessary to translate.

7. **SOCIOLOGY**   Estimate the sociological problems which
                     might accompany the end of the world.
                     Construct an experiment to test your theory.

8. **ENGINEERING** The disassembled parts of a high-powered
                     rifle have been placed on your desk. You
                     will also find an instruction manual, printed
                     in Swahili. In three minutes a hungry Bengal
                     Tiger will be admitted to the room. Take
                     whatever action you feel is appropriate. Be
                     prepared to justify your decision.

9. **ECONOMICS**   Develop a realistic plan for refining the
                     national debt. Trace the effects of your plan
                     on the following areas: cubism, the Donatist
                     controversy, the wave theory of light.
                     Outline a method for preventing these
                     effects. Criticise this method from all
                     possible points of view. Point out the
                     deficiencies in your point of view, as
                     demonstrated by your answer to the last
                     question.

10. **POLITICAL**   There is a red telephone on the desk beside
    SCIENCE   you. Start World War III. Report at length on
                     its socio-political effects, if any.

11. **EPISTEMOLOGY** Take a stand for or against truth. Prove the
                     validity of your position.

12. **PHYSICS**   Explain the nature of matter.

13. **PHILOSOPHY**   Sketch the development of human thought.
                     Estimate its significance. Compare with the
                     development of any other kind of thought.

14. **GENERAL**   Describe in detail. Be objective and specific.
    KNOWLEDGE

BUREAU OF SPEECH SERVICES

CAN YOU FOLLOW DIRECTIONS?

This is a timed test — You have three minutes **ONLY**.

1. Read everything carefully before doing anything.
2. Put your name in the upper right-hand corner of this paper.
3. Circle the 'NAME' in sentence two.
4. Draw five small squares in the upper left-hand corner.
5. Neatly put an 'X' in each square.
6. Put a circle around each square.
7. Sign your name under the title of this paper.
8. After the title write 'YES, YES, YES.'
9. Put a circle completely around sentence four.
10. Put an 'X' in the lowest left corner of this paper.
11. Draw a rectangle around the 'X' that you put down in sentence four.
12. Put a triangle around the 'X' that you put down for sentence ten.
13. On the back of this paper, multiply 703 by 66.
14. Loudly call out your first name when you get this far.
15. If you think that you have followed directions carefully to this point, call out, 'I HAVE.'
16. On the reverse side of this paper, add 8950 and 9805.
17. Put a circle around your answer, and then put a square around the circle.
18. In your normal speaking voice, count ten to one, backwards.
19. If you are the first person to reach this point, LOUDLY call out, 'I AM THE FIRST PERSON TO THIS POINT, AND I AM THE LEADER IN FOLLOWING DIRECTIONS.'
20. Punch three small holes in the top of this paper with your pencil point.
21. Underline all even numbers on the left side of this paper.
22. Put a square around each written-out number on this paper.
23. Loudly call out, 'I AM NEARLY FINISHED, I HAVE FOLLOWED DIRECTIONS.'
24. Now that you have finished everything carefully, do only sentences one and two.

A rope overhangs a pulley with a weight on one end and a monkey of the same weight on the other end.

The rope weighs 4 ozs. per foot and the monkey weighs as many pounds as its mother is years old.

The ages of the monkey and its mother add up to four years.

The monkey's mother is twice as old as the monkey was when the monkey's mother was half as old as the monkey will be when the monkey is three times as old as the monkey's mother was, when the monkey's mother was three times as old as the monkey.

The weight of the weight and the weight of the rope together are half as much again, as the difference between the weight of the rope and the weight of the monkey.

How long is the rope?

There are 5 houses, each with a different color, inhabited by men of different nationalities. The men own different pets, drink different drinks, and smoke different brands of cigarettes.

Facts

1. The Englishman lives in the red house.

2. The Spaniard owns the dog.

3. Coffee is drunk in the green house.

4. The Ukrainian drinks tea.

5. The green house is immediately to the right of the ivory house.

6. The Old Gold smoker owns snails.

7. Kools are smoked in the yellow house.

8. Milk is drunk in the middle house.

9. The Norwegian lives in the first house. (left)

10. The man who smokes Chesterfields lives in the house next to the one with the fox.

11. The Lucky Strike smoker drinks orange juice.

12. The Japanese smokes Parliaments.

13. Kools are smoked in the house next to the house where the horse is kept.

14. The Norwegian lives next to the blue house.

A. Who drinks water?
B. Who owns the zebra?

Six men, Andrews, Blaine, Colter, Doister, Ebert and Fisher are the only members eligible for the office of president, vice president and secretary in a certain organisation.

If:

Andrews won't be an officer unless Ebert is president,

Blaine won't serve if he outranks Colter,

Blaine won't serve with Fisher under any conditions,

Colter won't serve with both Ebert and Fisher,

Colter won't serve if Fisher is President or Blaine is secretary,

Doister won't serve with Colter or Ebert unless he outranks them,

Ebert won't be vice-president,

Ebert won't be secretary if Doister is an officer,

Ebert won't serve with Andrews unless Fisher serves too,

Fisher won't serve unless either he or Colter is president,

How can the three offices be filled?

President _____

Vice-President _____

Secretary _____

Grace, Helen and Mary were discussing their ages one day and, in the course of their conversation they made the following assertions.

Grace: I am twenty-two.
I am two years younger than Helen.
I am a year older than Mary.

Helen: I am not the youngest.
Mary and I are three years apart.
Mary is twenty-five.

Mary: I am younger than Grace.
Grace is twenty-three.
Helen is three years older than Grace.

It is, of course, too much to expect that three young women should be entirely truthful when speaking of their ages and, in the present instance, only two of the three statements made by each woman is true.

Deduce the age of each one:

Grace .... Helen .... Mary ....

DEFINE YOUR TERMS

THE BOSS
Leaps tall buildings in a single bound.
Is more powerful than a locomotive.
Is faster than a speeding bullet.
Walks on water.
Gives policy to God.

ESTIMATOR
Leaps short buildings in a single bound.
Is more powerful than a shunting engine.
Is just as fast as a speeding bullet.
Walks on water if sea is calm.
Talks with God.

ENGINEER
Leaps short buildings with a running start and favourable winds.
Is almost as powerful as a shunting engine.
Can shoot a speeding bullet.
Walks on water in an indoor swimming pool.
Talks with God if special request is approved.

PROJECT MANAGER
Makes high marks on the walls when trying to leap tall buildings.
Is run over by locomotives.
Can sometimes handle a gun without inflicting self-injury.
Dog-paddles.
Talks to animals.

SUPERINTENDENT
Runs into buildings.
Recognizes locomotives two out of three times.
Is not issued ammunition.
Can stay afloat with a life jacket.
Talks to walls.

PROJECT OFFICE MANAGER
Falls over doorsteps when trying to enter buildings.
Says 'Look at the choo-choo'.
Wets himself with a water pistol.
Plays in mud puddles.
Mumbles to himself.

THE SECRETARY
Lifts buildings and walks under them.
Kicks locomotives off the tracks.
Catches speeding bullets in her teeth and eats them.
Freezes water with a single glance.
She is God.

ENGINEERING DEFINITIONS
(From our Works Correspondent)

It has been found in the past that many people do not obtain the full meaning of articles containing engineering terms owing to their inability to understand them fully.

We are, therefore, enclosing this list of definitions to help the non-technically minded of our readers to obtain fuller enjoyment from their reading.

Machine   A mechanical device for the removal of redundant portions of the operator's anatomy. It is fitted with various lethal weapons known as tools.

Operator   A person suffering from the delusion that he controls the above machine. Chiefly employed in exhibiting grossly inflated wage packets to non-engineering friends.

Setter   An interesting animal kept by the management and trained to replace broken tools, etc. Is very docile when deprived of sleep.

Inspector   A survival of the Spanish Inquisition. Chief function is to weaken the operator's nerve, thus rendering him easy prey to the machine. This is accomplished by informing him that certain dimensions are undersize and, when adjusted, are then oversize by the same amount.

Ratefixer   An illiterate being whose mental processes cannot assimilate the fact that there are only 60 seconds to the minute.

Tool-grinder   One who can grind a cutting-edge in such a manner as to leave it in exactly the same condition as before.

Reamer   A device for producing various designs on a bore surface.

Gauge   An instrument made of metal which has the peculiar property of momentary expansion or contraction.

Storekeeper   Another name for a somnambulist.

Chargehand   Strict caution should be observed in dealing with this individual. From his frequent enquiries as to the number of hours you are working, he is probably connected with the Income Tax authorities.

Wage-packet	Delayed-action bombshell.
Scrap	See swarf.
Component	By-product of the manufacture of the above.
Millwright	A sort of comic who appears and reappears at irregular intervals.
Swarf	Staple product of engineering.
Labourer	This specimen with no ambition does nothing all day and stays overtime to finish it. Always missing when wanted. Very obliging about a week before Christmas.
Bonus	Latin name for a carrot dangled in front of a donkey.
Foreman	Very rarely seen except when you are filling in your football coupons.
Tap	Similar to a reamer only much more brittle.
Technical Offices	Dormitories provided for those individuals who have overworked themselves failing their examinations at tech.
Coolant Pump	A device so designed as to deluge the operator with oil or water when he is not looking.
Finish	An abstract term used by the Inspector and is something that is never good enough.
Bolt	A cylindrical piece of metal with helical screw on it that is either undersize or oversize.
Nut	Something that never fits on the above.
Location Diameter	A size which is never right and is always produced by another department.
Faulty Set-up	An accomplishment always achieved by the opposite shift.
Model	A standard of excellence achieved accidentally.
Drawing	Pictorial representation of a dream seen in a trance by a medium.
Draughtsman	Medium.
Drawing-office	Trance.

Military Intelligence

..... IS A HIGHLY REFINED ORGANIZATION OF OVERWHELMING GENERALITIES BASED ON VAGUE ASSUMPTIONS AND DEBATABLE FIGURES DRAWN FROM UNDISCLOSED ACTIVITIES PURSUED BY PERSONS OF DIVERSE MOTIVATION, DOUBTFUL RELIABILITY, AND QUESTIONABLE MENTALITY IN THE MIDST OF UNIMAGINABLE CONFUSION.

A COMPUTER SPECIALIST IS ONE WHO PASSES HIMSELF
OFF AS AN EXACTING EXPERT ON THE BASIS OF BEING
ABLE TO TURN OUT, AFTER INNUMERABLE DEBUGGING
SESSIONS, AN INFINITE SERIES OF INCOMPREHENSIBLE
ANSWERS CALCULATED WITH MICROMETRIC PRE-
CISION FROM VAGUE ASSUMPTIONS BASED ON DEBAT-
ABLE FIGURES TAKEN FROM INCONCLUSIVE DOCUMENTS
OF PROBLEMATICAL ACCURACY BY PERSONS OF
DUBIOUS RELIABILITY AND QUESTIONABLE MENTALITY
FOR THE PURPOSE OF ANNOYING AND CONFOUNDING A
HOPELESSLY DEFENSELESS DEPARTMENT THAT WAS
UNFORTUNATE ENOUGH TO HAVE ASKED FOR THE
INFORMATION.

'The typical auditor is a man past middle age, spare, wrinkled, intelligent, cold, passive, non-committal, with eyes like a cod fish, polite in contact but at the same time unresponsive, cold and damnably composed as a concrete post or a plaster of paris cast; a human petrification with a heart of feldspar and without charm of the friendly germ, minus bowels, passion or a sense of humor. Happily they never reproduce and all of them finally go to hell.'

AN ARCHITECT IS A MAN WHO KNOWS A VERY LITTLE ABOUT A GREAT DEAL AND KEEPS KNOWING LESS AND LESS ABOUT MORE AND MORE UNTIL HE KNOWS PRACTICALLY NOTHING ABOUT EVERY-THING.

AN ENGINEER IS A MAN WHO KNOWS A GREAT DEAL ABOUT VERY LITTLE AND WHO GOES ALONG KNOWING MORE AND MORE ABOUT LESS AND LESS UNTIL HE FINALLY KNOWS PRACTICALLY EVERY-THING ABOUT NOTHING.

A CONTRACTOR STARTS OUT KNOWING PRAC-TICALLY EVERYTHING, BUT ENDS UP KNOWING NOTHING ABOUT ANYTHING, DUE TO HIS ASSOCIA-TION WITH ARCHITECTS AND ENGINEERS.

ASTROLOGICAL SIGNS

AQUARIUS Jan 20 – Feb 18
You have an inventive mind and are inclined to be progressive. You lie a great deal. On the other hand, you are inclined to be careless and impractical, causing you to make mistakes over and over again. People think you are stupid.

PISCES Feb 19 – Mar 20
You have a vivid imagination and often think you are being followed by the CIA or FBI. You have a minor influence over your associates and people resent you for your flaunting it at your peers. You lack confidence and are generally a coward. Pisces people do horrible things to little animals.

ARIES Mar 21 – Apr 19
You are the pioneer type and hold most people in contempt. You are quick tempered, impatient and scornful of advice. You are not nice.

TAURUS Apr 20 – May 20
You are practical and persistent. You have a dogged determination and work like hell. Most people think you are stubborn and bullheaded. You are a communist.

GEMINI May 21 – June 20
You are a quick and intelligent thinker. People love you because you are bi-sexual. However, you are inclined to expect too much for too little. This means you are cheap. Geminis are known for committing incest.

CANCER June 21 – July 22
You are sympathetic and understanding to other people and their problems. They think you are a sucker. You are always putting things off. That is why you'll never amount to anything. Most welfare recipients are Cancer people.

LEO   July 23 – Aug 22
You consider yourself to be a born leader. Others think you are pushy. Most Leo people are bullies. You are vain and dislike honest criticism. Your arrogance is disgusting. Leo people are known thieves.

VIRGO   Aug 23 – Sept 22
You are the logical type and hate disorder. Your nit-picking is sickening to your friends. You are cold and unemotional and sometimes you fall asleep while making love. Virgos make good bus drivers.

LIBRA   Sept 23 – Oct 22
You are artistic and have a difficult time with reality. If you are a man, you are more than likely queer. Chances for employment along this line and monetary gains are excellent. All Libras die of venereal disease.

SCORPIO   Oct 23 – Nov 21
You are shrewd in business and cannot be trusted. You shall achieve the pinnacles of success because you totally lack ethics. Most Scorpio people are murdered.

SAGITTARIUS   Nov 22 – Dec 21
You are optimistic and enthusiastic. You have a reckless tendency to rely on luck, since you lack talent. The majority of Sagittarians are drunks and dope fiends. People laugh at you a great deal.

CAPRICORN   Dec 22 – Jan 19
You are conservative and afraid of taking risks. You don't do anything and are lazy. There has never been a Capricorn of any importance. Capricorns should avoid standing too long, as they tend to take root and become trees.

GLOSSARY OF TERMS FOR USE
IN MODIFICATION CONTROL CORRESPONDENCE

Programme

Any assignment that cannot be completed by one telephone call.

Expedite

To confound the confusion with commotion.

Co-ordinate

A person who has a desk between two expeditors.

Consultant Specialist

Someone to pass the job or query on to.

Clarification

To fill in the background with so much detail that the foreground goes underground.

To give the picture

A long, confused and inaccurate statement to a newcomer.

To activate

To make carbons and add more names to the memo.

Note and initial

Spreading the responsibility.

We are making a survey

We need more time to think of an answer.

We will advise you in due course

If we figure it out we will let you know.

With modifications

Sent out in pieces and full of alterations; put it together yourself.

Under consideration

We have lost the file.

Under active consideration

We are trying to find the file.

For attention and necessary action

It's up to you to get rid of it to somebody else.

Let's get together on this

It's got me beat. How about you?

Implement the programme

Increase the staff and make the job bigger.

We are making exhaustive enquiries

You'll have to wait a long time for the answer to this.

Thank you for your esteemed enquiry

We have had about enough of your trouble.

A reliable source

Someone you have just met.

An informed source

The person who told the person that you have just met.

Unimpeachable source

The comedian who started the rumour in the first place.

COMMON MARKET MOTORING

In anticipation of our impending entry in the Common Market we offer motorists this lighthearted glossary of motoring terms

Indicators	Die Blinkenlightenmittickenfurturnen
Bonnet	Der Fingerpinscher und Kopfchopper
Exhaust Pipe	Das Spitzenpoppenbangentuben
Speedometer	Der Egobooster und Lineschootinbackeruppen
Clutch	Das Kupplinverk mit Schlippen und Schtinken
Air Horns	Der Vatderhellvosdat Klaxonfanfaren
Puncture	Das Pflatt mit Dammundblasten
Learner Driver	Dumkopff mit Elplatz
GT	Der Ellovagi mit Dumkopfblonde
Estate Car	Der Schnogginwagen mit Bagseroomfurrompininderback
Mini	Der Buzzboxen mit Traffikveerinfistschakenundfingerraisin
Petrol	Das Koslijooze fur Geddingreezoffendentrousen
Motor Club	Der Meetinghaus fur Wagennatterinelbowraisin und Chaddenupziebirds
Magistrate	Der Khortfuhror mit Schauten 'Zweihunnermarks und Lizenzendorzen'
Parking Meter	Das Tannerpinscher Klockenwerks
Windscreen Wipers	Das Flippenfloppenmuckschpredun und Schticken
Crossroads	Das Kussundschvearingstrassen
Roundabout	Das Eeoohezitatzisschlost
T Junction	Das Vergutnessakedontgostraitonnenkorner
Power Brakes	Die Schtoppinwerks mit Edbangenondervindscreen
Level Crossing	Die Flattenbitundpuffpufftracken
Low Bridge	Das Makengrössenbus in Singeldekker
Rear Engined	Die Frauwasserinderpetroltankenputten
Front Engined	Die Fraupetrolindiewasserverherkeputten
Gear Lever	Das Kangeroohpanpickenschticke
Constable	Der Kopper
W.P.C.	Skirtenkopperfrau
Police Cadet	Kopperkinder
Chief Constable	Koppergott

Sergeant	Dumthumpenkopper
Desk Sergeant	Buckenschreibenkopper
C.I.D.	Knockeroffenschnatcher
Police Frogman	Unterseekopper
River Police	Gordolphinkopper
Police Helicopter	Kopperchoppur
Flying Squad	Fliegelkoppergang
Police Station	Koppernickenhaus
Station Officer	Oberkoppernickenhausfuhrer
Traffic Patrol	Autobahnspiedenschnatchenkopper
R.T. Car	Automitkrackeilspielenwagon
Lightweight Motorcycle	Noddischplutter
Duty Boots	Klumperkraschors
Refreshments	Noschenkupperbelch
Police Dog	Schniffelrippenhund
Time Off	Nein
Truncheon	Yobbenschmasser
Traffic Duty	Autobahnenbuggeruppen
Police Helmet	Koppertopper
'Hold for Questioning'	Strangelthumpemschmash
Crowd Control	Volksthumpen
Handcuffs	Mittenknipper
'Physically Restrain'	Maimenkrippel
Cell	Gerthumpenbox
Anti-Police Informant	Kopperschoppur
Mounted Policeman	Gerdobbinkopper
Police Station Steps	Koppernickenhaustrippen
Cell Steps	Trippenschmashgersteppen
Self Defense	Gerbollokschmashen
Dog Van Policeman	Autohunderkopper
Disorderly Crowd	Gruppenyobschwein
Crowd Control	Gruppenruptur
Student	Kleverdikkenyob
Pig	Englischerkopper
Enquiries	Pokenprie und thumpen

CARTOON TIME

IRELANDS FIRST
BIONIC MAN

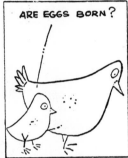

WHAT IS IT?

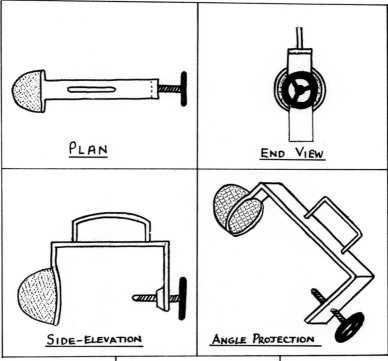

PLAN

END VIEW

SIDE-ELEVATION

ANGLE PROJECTION

NOTE - NOT TO SCALE

DIMENSIONS [EXAMPLE]
HEIGHT 12" x 24" LONG

SUGGESTED PRICE
£ 25-00

MATERIALS - STAINLESS STEEL
WIRE MESH   LEATHER

REMARKS   OTHER SIZES TO BE
KEPT ON STOCK

ASK TO SEE AGENTS PHOTOGRAPH FOR METHOD OF USE

PTO

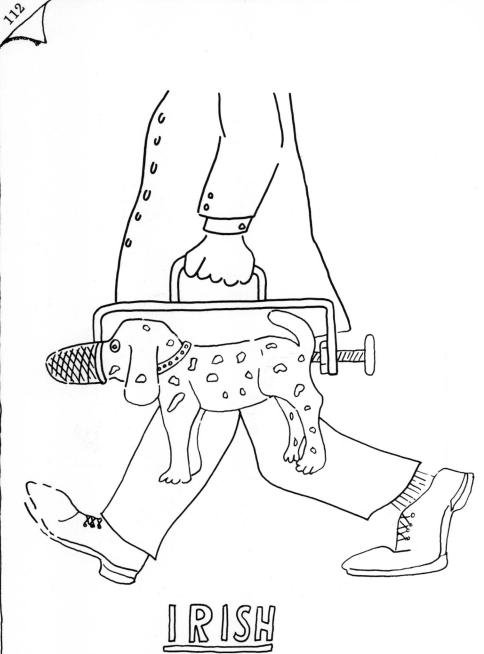

IRISH
DOG CARRIER

LAB REPORT NO. <u>767</u>

DATE: 25·10·78

   DEAR MR Smith.

   YOUR X-RAY PLATES HAVE BEEN RETURNED AND I AM
PLEASED TO TELL YOU THAT I THINK I HAVE FOUND YOUR
TROUBLE.

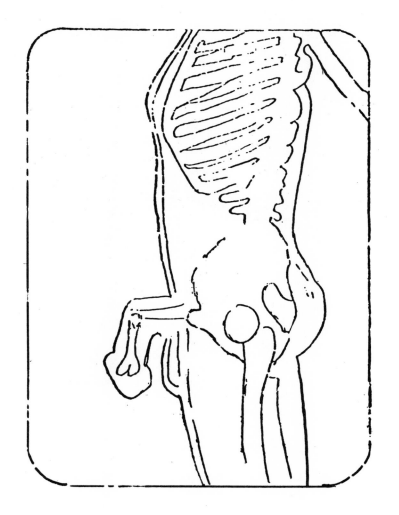

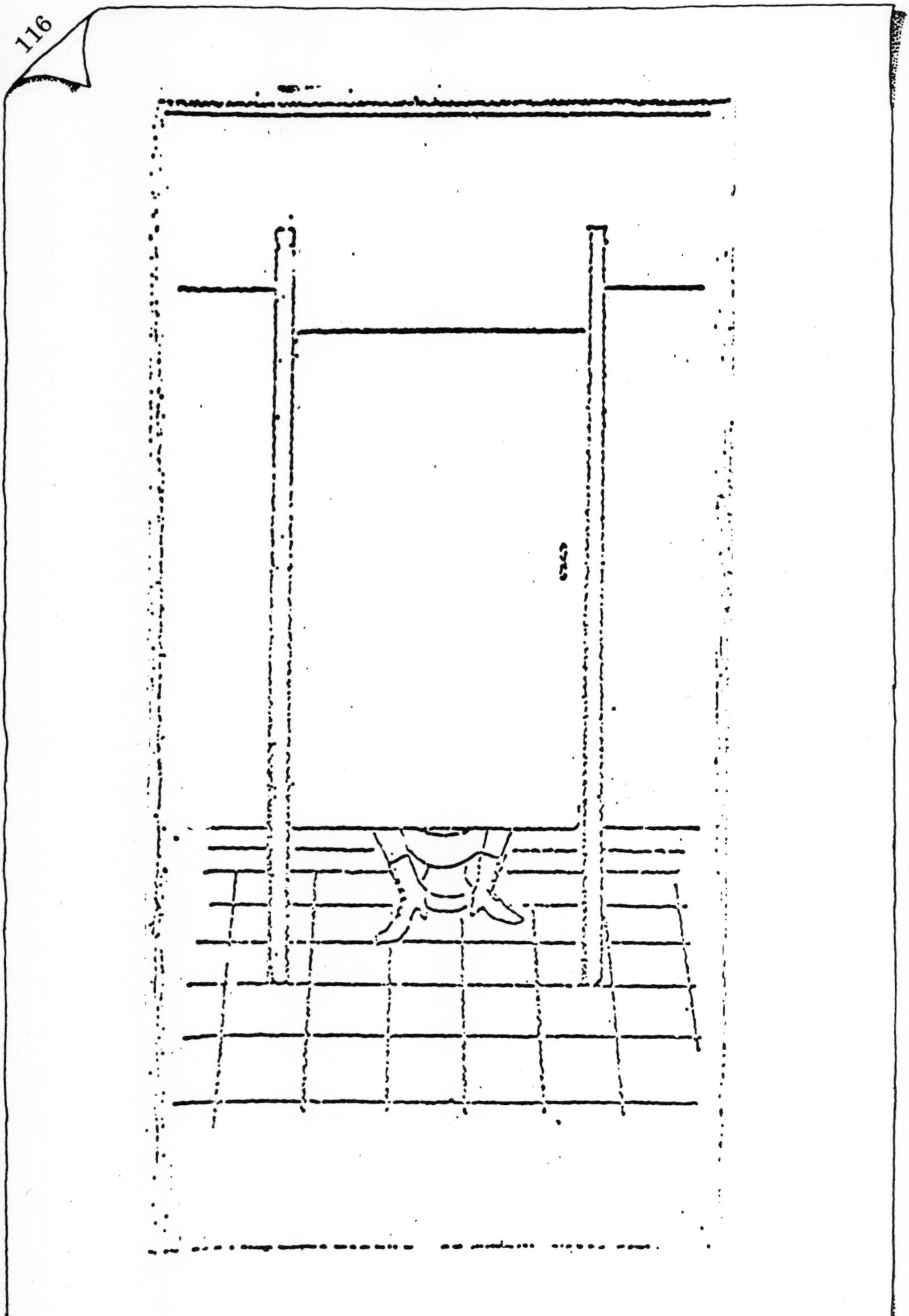

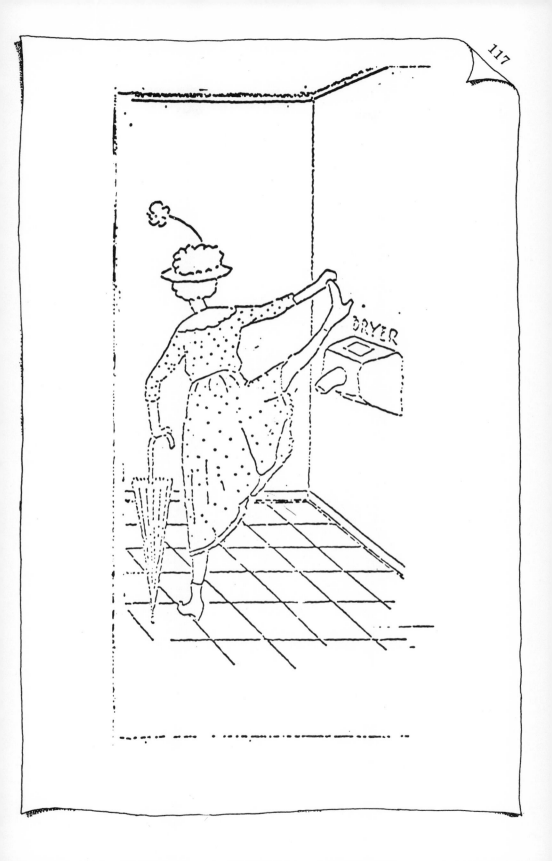

"SYSTEM BEEN DOWN LONG?"

'WORST CASE OF DIARRHOEA
I'VE EVER SEEN'

"NO YOU CAN'T TOUCH IT, YOU'VE BROKEN YOURS OFF ALREADY!!

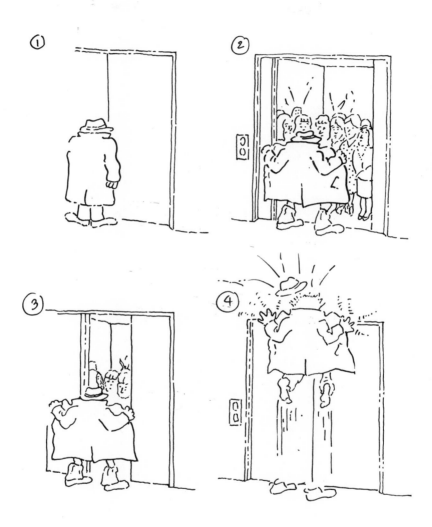

THE
FLASHER

THE MORNING MAIL

10 Downing Street,
London

Dear Sir,

You are no doubt aware of the serious situation that
has arisen in the Falkland Islands and the resulting
drastic repercussions that have compelled the Government
to take the necessary action to protect the sovereignty
of these Islands.

The Government are urgently compiling a list of people
whom we think would be of the calibre to undertake arduous,
dangerous and essentially secret duties on our behalf; your
name has been put forward as a suitable candidate.

There are few options open to the Government but it
is proposed that we infiltrate the Falkland Islands with
such stealth and speed that the Argentinian invaders would
be taken completely by surprise. Initially one school of
thought is to disguise a group of volunteers as penguins so
that they may land on the Island without arousing too much
suspicion. These penguins would then reconnoitre the island
causing as much damage as possible by sabotaging military
installations, e.g. dropping penguins' eggs down gun turrets,
etc., and to set up road blocks by means of general gathering
and strutting about as penguins are prone to do.

This is where you come in; we have studied your statistics
and feel that you are the ideal size and shape for one of
these penguins. It would, of course, mean that you would not
be registered under the War Department but the Ministry of
Fisheries; other than this we can see no overwhelming obstacles
to this venture.

Perhaps you would be kind enough to report to me as soon
as possible so that you may be measured for your outfit and
also change your diet to fish as soon as possible.

Yours faithfully,
Ministry of Emergencies and Contingencies

Dear Sir,

I wish to apply for an operation to make me sterile. My reasons are numerous and after being married for seven years and having seven children, I have come to the conclusion that contraceptives are totally useless.

After getting married, I was told to use the "Rhythm Method" but, despite trying the Tango and the Samba, my wife fell pregnant and I ruptured myself doing the Cha Cha Cha; apart from which, where do you get a band at five o'clock in the morning?

A doctor suggested we use the "Safe Period". At the time we were living with the in-laws and we had to wait three weeks for a safe period when the house was empty - needless to say this didn't work.

A lady of several years' experience informed us that if we made love whilst breast feeding we would be alright. It's hardly Newcastle Brown Ale, but I did finish up with a clear skin, silky hair and the wife pregnant.

Another old wives' tale was that if my wife jumped up and down after intercourse it would prevent pregnancy. After the constant breast feeding from my earlier attempt, if my wife jumped up and down she would finish up with two black eyes and eventually knock herself unconscious.

I asked the chemist about the sheath. The chemist demonstrated how easy it was to use, so I bought a packet. My wife fell pregnant again, which doesn't surprise me, as I fail to see how a Durex stretched over the thumb, as the chemist showed me, can prevent babies.

She was then supplied with the coil and, after several unsuccessful attempts to fit it, we realised we had got a left hand thread and my wife is definitely a right hand screw.

The Dutch cap came next. We were very hopeful of this as it did not interfere with our sex life at all but, alas, it gave my wife severe headaches. We were given the largest size available but it was still too tight across her forehead.

Finally we tried the pill. At first it kept falling out, then I realised we were doing it wrong. My wife then started putting it between her knees thus preventing me getting anywhere near her. This did work for a while, until the night she forgot the pill.

You must appreciate my problem. If this operation is unsuccessful I will have to revert to oral sex, although just talking about it can never be a substitute for the real thing.

Yours faithfully,

Mr. 'X'

Dear Marjorie Proops,

    I would be grateful if you could advise me on the following problem.

    I am 32 years old and have two brothers, one is working for the South Yorkshire County Council and is an ardent Sheffield Wednesday supporter, the other is in Durham Jail serving six years for rape and larceny.

    My father is a fine gentleman living off the earnings of my two sisters who are on the streets, holding down good positions in the West End. My mother is pregnant to our next door neighbour and, in view of this, my father has refused to marry her.

    Recently I met a lovely charming girl who is an ex-prostitute; sweet, simple and a mother of three beautiful children. We plan to marry soon.

    The problem is should I tell her about my brother who is a Sheffield Wednesday supporter.

                     Signed:

                     DESPERATE

Middlehurst Home for
Elderly Ladies,
Middleton,
Leeds 10.

17th January, 1971

Thomas Andrews, Esq.,
The Rotary Club of Leeds,

Dear Mr. Andrews,

I am writing to thank you for the lovely transistor radio
you so kindly sent me at Christmas-time. It is all the more
wonderful that an absolute stranger like yourself should
remember an old lady such as me.

I am 80 years old and have been in this home for 16 years.
We are very kindly treated but the lonely hours are hard
to beat.

My room-mate, Mrs. James, has a radio but will never let
me listen to it and even switches it off when I come into the
room. Well, now I have one of my own.

My son and daughter are very nice and come to see me once
a month but I know they only visit me from a sense of duty.
This is why your gift is all the more wonderful and thrilling
to me as it was given out of compassion for a fellow human
being. Bless you.

Today Mrs. James' radio went wrong and she asked if she
could listen to mine. I told her to bugger off.

Yours sincerely,

VALENTINE GREETINGS;

To My Ever Loving Wife:

During the past year I have attempted to seduce you 365 times. I have succeeded 12 times. This averages once every 30 days. The following is a list of reasons for which I did not succeed.

We'll wake the children   7

It's too hot   15

It's too cold   5

Too tired   39

It's too late   16

It's too early   22

Pretending sleep   60

Windows open,
   neighbors might see   9

Backache   16

Toothache   2

I'm too full   4

Giggles   4

Not in the mood   21

Watched the late show   7

Baby crying   19

Watched the early show   5

Mud pack   5

Grease on face   21

Reading in bed   7

You're too drunk   5

Reading Sunday paper   52

Headache   10

Do you think we could improve our record this coming year????????????????

PLEASE BE MY VALENTINE,

Hopefully
Your ever Loving Husband

130

CIVIL DEFENCE PROGRAMME

CIVIL DEFENCE COMMITTEE

Dear

Under the direction of the Civil Defence Programme, we are entering into extensive training to organize both civilian and industrial Corps for the training purpose of fire-fighting in the event of the danger of Atomic Air Raids becoming imminent.

As a Citizen whose loyalty to the country is unquestioned, we believe that we may count on you to co-operate fully and we have, therefore, taken the liberty of appointing you Atomic Air Raid Warden for the District of Dronfield.

Training will be confirmed later on but will be confined to three nights a week for six months.

Stated below is a list of equipment necessary for the Atomic Warden which will be issued to you at the first meeting and must be brought with you at all subsequent meetings:-

EQUIPMENT

1. Respirator.
2. Stirrup pump to be carried over right shoulder.
3. Extending ladder to be carried over the left shoulder.
4. Long shovel to be carried under the right arm.
5. Rake to be carried in the left hand.
6. Whistle hanging from lanyard to be carried in mouth.
7. Belt to be round the waist with ten hooks for carrying sand bags and four pails of water.
8. Axe to be carried in belt.
9. Two wet blankets to be slung round neck.
10. Tin helmet with brim turned up to carry extra water.
11. Flashlight to be carried round neck.
12. Extra sand to be carried in all available pockets.
13. Ship's anchor to be dropped in case Warden wants to stop.
14. Spare pea for whistle to be carried in left ear.
15. Broom to be inserted in only place left, so the Warden may sweep the floor as he progresses.

We hope to have your kind co-operation in this matter.

Please accept the thanks of the Committee in anticipation of your part in this enterprise which we feel is so vital to the best interests of us all.

May/June 1973

F.C.D'Arcy-Smythe
Colonel Commanding,
Headquarters.

A LETTER
FROM AN IRISHWOMAN
TO HER SON

Dear Son,

   This is your dear old mother writing to you. There is a lot of interesting news since you left. It's wet but not as wet as when it was real wet. I'm writing this slow because I know you can't read fast. Excuse the writing I had an accident, burnt my fingers in boiling water. I should have felt the water before I put my fingers in it. I'm feeling better since you went away: Went to the doctor and got a wonderful medicine for my deafness. I took a dose on Friday night and it was so good I heard from Uncle Hughie in Australia on the Saturday morning. I feel 25 years younger and your father is delighted. Your brother Ernie came in crying from school this evening because all his pals have new clothes: We can't afford to buy him a new outfit so we are going to buy him a new hat and let him look out the window.

   We had a row with the electric light company; it ended in a draw: we got no light and they got no money. It is very dark but not as dark as when it was real dark. We are hard up son, send us a few quid - it will only cost you five pence.

   Our neighbours the Browns started to keep pigs and we only got the wind of them this morning. Friday night was wet, we went to bed early. Mr. Higgins got his appendix out and a new kitchen sink in. The cat had four kittens in your father's hat. I put them in a box in case they grew up round shouldered. The undertaker called and said that if the last instalment isn't paid on your mother-in-law, up she'd come. Your father has worms and has gone fishing. We heard from your cousin that Annie passed away, your old Grannie died and Fanny married the butcher, so now you have no Annie, no Grannie and no Fannie.

   Your father has a good job now, first in 10 years. We are a great deal better off than we were. Your father gets £10 every Thursday as we do a bit of fixing up. We bought one of the new fangled things they call bathrooms. You hear tell of them in some houses. It is put in by a man called a plumber. On one side of the room is a big long thing, what you used to feed the pigs in before you went away. We jump into that and wash all over. But near that is a small one they call a sink. That is for light washing such as hands and face. Ah! but over in the corner is the nicest contraption of all. You put one foot in and wash it clean, then pull a little chain and you get fresh water for the other foot. Two covers came with it and we hadn't any use for them in the bathroom, so I'm using one as a bread board and the other has a hole in it so we framed your grandad's picture. They sent us a big roll of writing paper with it, this is what I'm using now Son to write to you. Take care of yourself.

                Your Mammy.

P L A Y G I R L   i n c

CONSOLIDATED BUILDINGS
1167 WALL STREET
NEW YORK
NY 10008 USA

CENTERFOLD DIVISION
Telephone (212) 943-6060

Dear MR ASHTON

Your name has been submitted to us with your
photograph, and I regret to inform you that we
will be unable to use your body in our center
fold.

On the scale of 0-10, your body was rated 2 by
our panel of women ranging in ages from 60-75
years. We tried to assemble a panel in the age
bracket of 25-30 years but we could not stop
them laughing long enough to reach a decision.

Should the taste of women ever change so
drastically that bodies such as yours would be
appreciated in our center-fold, you will be
notified by this office. In the meantime, do not
call us - we'll call you.

Sympathetically

A. Ericsson

Amanda Ericsson
EDITOR
Playgirl Inc Magazine

PS   We do commend you for your unusual pose.
Were you wounded in the War - or do you
ride a bike a lot?

Dear Friend:

This chain letter was started by a woman like yourself in hopes of bringing relief to tired, discontented women.

Unlike most chain letters, this one does not cost anything. Just send a copy of this letter to five of your friends who are equally tired. Then bundle up your husband and send him to the woman whose name is on top of the list.

When your name comes to the top of the list, you will receive 16,478 men - some of whom ought to be dandies.

Have faith! Do not break the chain! One woman broke the chain and got her own husband back.

Sincerely,

P.S. At the time of writing a friend of mine has received 183 men. They buried her yesterday but it took three undertakers 36 hours to take the smile off her face.

Dear Ann Landers

    After 5 years of marriage I am finaly convinced I am married to a sex maniac

    My problem is this He insists on making love to me at all hours of the day, regardless of what I am doing, —— the dishes, making the bed, or tending the children What do you suggest?

        Sincerely yours

        Matilda Snodgrass

P.S. Please pardon this jerky writing

SLIGHTLY CONFIDENTIAL

A.F. off/preg/confes/xxi
(Modified for India)

PRO-FORMA FOR USE BY WIVES OF SOLDIERS SERVING OVERSEAS.

(Obtainable from all Post Offices, Labour Exchanges and
Anti-Natal Clinics)
Issued pursuant to (s.69). U.K. Troops (prohibition of Leave) and Allied
Forces Act of 1945.

STRIKE OUT WORDS NOT APPLICABLE.

My dearest/darling/loving/beloved husband,

I hope this finds you in the pink as it leaves me.
This will come as a great shock to you but do not do anything rash
                Terrible surprise   to yourself
                                          I wouldn't do

I do not know how to say it but I have had a baby.
                tell you   fell for a child
                                    got in trouble (again?)

    I met a Canadian/American/Dutchman/Pole/Free Frenchman/Greek/
Italian/Egyptian/Czech/Yugoslav/Scandinavian/German Prisoner/cheeky
old thing/man in a pub/nasty beggar/nice boy/Airman/Soldier/Sailor/
dirty dog and we had a few/many drinks at

. . . .

I do know what happened, but of course you can guess what happened.
don't

I was sober. He (did not) force (d) me. It all happened so quickly.
    drunk   slowly

I did like it. It only happened once . . . . times
did not   twice

Please forgive me. I do not suppose you can forget it.
      divorce me   forgive me

Please give me my freedom. I love you. You know I was always in love
        another chance   him   never   with
                                                    you.

You have always treated me fair. I will have it adopted.
      never   won't

                              Your broken hearted wife
P.S. It was on the common   ever loving
            up the back passage   unfaithful
            in the kitchen   lonely hearted
            in a taxi   loving
            dark
            wonderful   Signed . . . .
                                  (Insert crosses to suit your own
                                  taste in this space)

PARIS HOUSE MASSAGE PARLOUR LTD.

Paris House
300 Kennedy Street
Winnipeg, Manitoba
R3c OL7

Ph. 942-6705

Dear Mr. Davenport,

First of all let me thank you for the prompt
payment of your last bill. You have always been
one of our preferred clients through our long
relationship and I am sure that you will continue
to be one. The girls are always very excited when
they find out that "Bertie" is coming for a visit.

Now I must apologize for an error that we made on
your last statement. We inadvertently overcharged
you. Please see the attached corrected statement
and our enclosed refund.

Yours sincerely,
Paris House Limited
Per:

R. Lancaster
Credit Manager

RL/1f

PARIS HOUSE
Where the customer comes first

A.G. Davenport
170 Slater Ave.
Winnipeg, Man.
R2G ON8

Item	Date	Charge	Attendant	Net Charge
a.	09/03	22.50	Olga	22.50
a.	09/12	22.50	Svetlana	22.50
f.	09/20	31.95	Brucie	31.95
k.	10/09	35.00	Sally Bumshot	35.00
m.	10/22	43.00	Natasha	40.00
a.	11/14	22.50	Olga	22.50
n.	11/19	40.00	Annie Position	40.00
g.	11/29	37.50	Don Ho	37.50
			Total	$251.95
			Man. S.T. 5%	12.60
			Total	$264.55
			Paid	$274.55
			Credit	$10.00

Legend
a. massage (basic)
b. massage (feathers)
c. massage (leather)
d. bondage (½ hr. +?)
e. dutch treat
f. rubber ducky plus
g. drums of heaven
h. Ralph
i. Ralph with whips
j. water bed
k. animal tendency
l. the house special
m. Zorba's revenge
n. 69 was a good year

Dear Mom and Dad:

   Since arriving at college, I've been remiss in writing and I apologize. Please forgive me. I want to bring you up-to-date, but before reading any further - please sit down. I repeat, <u>DO NOT</u> read any further unless you are sitting down.

   Now the news. I'm Okay now. The skull fracture and concussion I got while jumping out the dormitory window during the fire have healed. I spent two weeks in the hospital but the stitches come out tomorrow and I can see almost normal and only get the dizzy spells and headaches once or twice a day now.

   Fortunately, the fire and my jump were witnessed by the attendant at a gas station and he was the one who called the fire department and the ambulance. He also visited me in the hospital and as I had no place to stay after the fire, he was kind enough to invite me to share his apartment. Actually, it's just a basement room and though small, it's cute.

   He's a very fine person and we have fallen deeply in love and want to get married. We have not set an exact date but it will be before my pregnancy starts to show.

   Yes, Mom and Dad, I'm pregnant. I know how thrilled you'll be to know you'll be grandparents and will welcome the baby and give it the same love and devotion you gave me as a child. The reason for the delay in our marriage is that my boyfriend has a minor infection which prevents him from passing the premarital bloodtest and this is some-what complicated by the fact that I've caught it too.

   I know that you will welcome Clem into the family with open arms. He is a wonderful human being and although not well educated, he is very ambitious. He is of a different race and religion than ours, but I know that your natural warmth and fairness will not permit you to become biased.

   Now that I've brought you up-to-date, I want to say there was no fire in my dormitory, no skull fracture or concussion. I was not in the hospital. I'm not pregnant, not engaged or in love, not infected and there is no boyfriend in my life. However, I am getting a "D" in history and an "F" in science and I want you to view these marks in their proper perspective.

Signed

YOUR LOVING DAUGHTER

SEVERN–TRENT WATER AUTHORITY

Circular No. 23/DSMA/59763/2a   Date as Postmark

The Occupier,

re: GENERAL RATES AND WATER
CHARGES

Dear Sir,

I am required to inform you that under Section 97 of the TOWN & COUNTY PLANNING ACT, 1951 (as amended 1954) you are in EXCESS of the quota of water allocated to your residence, I.E. 540 gallons per month.

THE COUNCIL INSPECTOR informs us that this is due to OVER USE OF W.C. FACILITIES.

As from April, 1980 the extra water will be charged for in the following manner:-

A METER will be installed, free of charge, on your W.C. Cistern (of British Standard Design) to register the number of times the W.C. is flushed.

The new sliding scale of Water Rates No. 3/A is applicable for this installation. As you are the first area to come under this scheme you have been allocated 65 free flushes per month before installation and operation of the meter. Thereafter, each flush will be charged at the rate of 1p (one pence) for the first 10 (ten) flushes, 3p (three pence) for the next 10 (ten) flushes, and thereafter at the rate of 5p (five pence) per flush.

Our Department is at your disposal for the next three months for any problems you may have on this matter.

Yours faithfully,

R. SOLE.
Chief Sewerage Statistician - Mains

A firm in Germany ordered coffee from an American firm and while the coffee was en route a few bags split open, making it possible for rats to nest in them. The Germans sent the following letter to the U.S.:

Schentlemens:

Der last 2 packeteeches ve got from you of Kaffee vas mit rattschidt gemidt. Der Kaffee maybe gute enuff, but dur ratt durds schboils der taste. Ve did not see der rattschidt in der samples vich you sent us. It takes so much time to pik der ratt durds from der Kaffee, dats its hardly wart it. Ve order der Kaffee clean and you schipt schidt mixt mit it. It vas mistake ja? Ve like you to schip us der Kaffee in vun sack and der ratt schidt in anudder – den ve mix it to suit der customer. Write blease if vs shouldt schip der schidt bek and keep der Kaffee or if vs shouldt keep der schidt and schip der Kaffee bek, or schip der whole schidden vorks bek.

Ve vant to do right in dis matter, but ve dont like all dis rattschidt bizniss.

> *Mitt mich respekts*
>
> *Karl Gunmenschidt*

EXAMPLES OF UNCLEAR WRITING

Sentences taken from actual letters received by the Welfare Department in application for support.

1. *I am forwarding my marriage certificate and six children. I had seven but one died which was baptized on a half sheet of paper.*

2. *I am writing the Welfare Department to say that my baby was born two years old. When do I get my money?*

3. *Mrs. Jones has not had any clothes for a year and has been visited regularly by the clergy.*

4. *I cannot get sick pay. I have six children. Can you tell me why?*

5. *I am glad to report that my husband who is missing is dead.*

6. *This is my eighth child, what are you going to do about it?*

7. *Please find out for certain if my husband is dead. The man I an now living with can't eat or do anything until he knows.*

8. *I am very much annoyed to find that you have branded my son illiterate. This is a dirty lie, as I was married a week before he was born.*

9. *In answer to your letter, I have given birth to a son weighing ten pounds. I hope this is satisfactory.*

10. *I am forwarding marriage certificate and my three children; one of which is a mistake as you can see.*

11. *My husband got his project cut off two weeks ago and I haven't had any relief since.*

12. *Unless I get my husband's money pretty soon, I will be forced to lead an immortal life.*

13. *You have changed my little boy to a girl. Will this make a difference?*

14. *I have no children as yet, as my husband is a truck driver and works night and day.*

15. *In accordance with your instructions, I have given birth to twins in the enclosed envelope.*

16. *I want money as quick as I can get it, I have been in bed with the doctor for two weeks and he doesn't do me any good. If things don't improve, I will have to send for another doctor.*

NORTH SEA GAS

These are genuine extracts from letters received by the Gas Board.

Complaints regarding placing of appliances and meters etc.

'Can you move the meter so it won't cause an obstruction in my passage.'

'The electric man did it through the floorboards, but your man put it in my front passage where everyone can see it.'

'I don't like it so much in the kitchen as I did in the show room window.'

Leakages

'Since you put a new pipe from the mains to our house, me and my husband dread going to bed because of a slight discharge. We think there is a leak just after it enters.'

'I told my husband it was safe to leave it in all night, but he won't. If he comes to the showroom like I did, can the lady satisfy him behind the counter and talk him out of it.'

General

'I was told mine is no good but if it is altered I can get the North sea in.'

'I have heard there are two ways you can have it and it worked out cheaper the more you get if you have it the other way.'

'I am not satisfied with an apprentice so will you send a man to do it properly.'

'My wife will be ready for your man if you will let her know when he is coming on a postcard.'

'I will try to pay before the end of the month because my husband will be surprised if you cut it off without telling him.'

'It has got slack with use and my husband can't make it right, no matter how he tries so for the time being we are making do with an old gas ring.'

'My slit is not blocked now but your men made an awful mess banging their tools on the wall.'

'Since I made arrangements with your salesman I am having a baby and would like to change it for a drying cabinet.'

'My neighbour has a bigger one than we had, it makes a difference to her water when she fills the bath.'

'My husband was under the impression I was getting it at reduced rates but your salesman didn't use his head and got me into trouble.'

'It is about time your workmen came back to fill the hole because we are fed up of having it in the street, it is a big attraction and we are getting children by the dozen.'

'The woman who is after the house said she is not keen on it. Can your man stand by to take it out before she comes.'

LANGUAGE AND THE MOTORIST

These are genuine extracts from Motor Claim Forms received by a large Insurance Office in London

The accident was due to the other man narrowly missing me.

I collided with a stationary tramcar coming in the opposite direction.

I left my Austin 7 outside, but I came out later, to my amazement, there was an Austin 12.

To avoid collision I ran into the other car.

There were plenty of lookers-on but no witnesses.

The water in my radiator accidentally froze at midnight.

I was scraping my nearside on the bank when the accident happened.

I collided with a stationary tree.

There was no damage done to the car as the gatepost will testify.

Accident was due to the road bending.

The other man altered his mind and I had to run into him.

I told the idiot what he was and went on.

One wheel went into the ditch. My foot jumped from brake to accelerator pedal, leapt across the road to the other side and jumped into the trunk of a tree.

A cow wandered into my car, I was afterwards informed that the cow was half witted.

She suddenly saw me, lost her head, and we met.

I was taking a friend home and keeping two yards from each lamp post which were in a straight line. Unfortunately there was a bend in the road bringing the right hand lamp post in line with the other and, of course, I landed in a ditch.

If the other driver had stopped a few yards behind himself, it would not have happened.

I bumped into a shop window and sustained injuries to my wife.

I misjudged a lady crossing the street.

Coming home I drove into the wrong house and collided with a tree I haven't got.

I can't give details of the accident as I was somewhat concussed at the time.

Wilful damage was done to the upholstery by rats.

I blew my horn but it would not work as it was stolen.

A lamp post bumped into my car, damaging it in two places.

The car in front stopped suddenly and I crashed gently into the luggage grid.

The other car collided with me, without giving warning of his intention.

I unfortunately ran over a pedestrian and the old gentleman was taken to hospital, much regretting the circumstances.

I thought the side window was down but it was up, as I found out when I put my head through it.

I consider neither vehicle was to blame. But if either vehicle was to blame it was the other one.

I looked for the sign but the more I looked the more I couldn't find it.

TEA BREAK
TALES

THE HALLOWEEN PARTY

A couple was invited to a masked halloween party and the wife got costumes for both of them. On the night of the party she developed a terrible headache and told her husband to go without her. He protested, but she said that all she was going to do was take a couple of aspirins and go to bed and there was no need for his good time to be spoiled by not attending. So he got into his costume and off he went.

The wife, after sleeping soundly for about an hour, awoke without a sign of pain and, as it was just a little after nine, she decided to go to the party. As her husband didn't know what kind of costume she was wearing, she thought it would be a good idea to slip into the party and observe how he acted when she wasn't around.

This she did and as soon as she joined the party the first person she spied was her husband, cavorting around on the dance floor, dancing with first one girl and then another – having a little feel here and there. So the wife sidled up to him and being rather seductive herself, he left his partner standing high and dry and devoted his attention to the new girl that had just arrived. She let him go as far as he wished (naturally) and finally he whispered a little proposition in her ear. She agreed and they went out to one of the cars parked nearby . . . etc., etc., etc.

Just before the unmasking at midnight she slipped away, went home and got into bed wondering what kind of an explanation her husband would make as to his behaviour. He arrived home about 1.30 a.m. and came right into the bedroom to see how she was. She was sitting up in bed reading and asked, 'What kind of time did you have?' He said, 'Oh, the same old thing. You know I never have a good time when you aren't around.' Then she asked, 'Did you dance much?' and he replied, 'Well, I'll tell you, I never danced a dance. When I got there Peter Jones, Bill Brown and some of the other fellows were also on their own. So we went into the back and played poker but, I'll tell you one thing, that fellow I loaned my costume to sure had a great time.'

A big business man was sitting at the bar drinking beer when a girl came in and sat on a stool next to him. He looked her over and started a conversation. He soon propositioned her and offered her £500 to spend the weekend with him at his home. Thinking how nice the £500 would be, she accepted. After the weekend was over and they started home, she asked him for the money and he said he'd post a cheque for the amount. The cheque arrived, but it was only for £250. So she decided to call on him at his office. It was full of people and not wanting to embarrass him she said: 'In regard to that house you rented, I only received half the rent.' The man catching on said: 'Oh yes, the house. Well, in the first place, you didn't tell me it had been used. In the second place, it was too big and, in the third place, there was no heat.' So she replied, saying: 'In the first place you didn't ask me if it had been used. In the second place it wasn't too big, you didn't have enough furniture to fill it, and in the third place, there was plenty of heat, you didn't know how to turn it on.' She got the other £250.

THE GASTRONOMICAL BEAN STORY

Once upon a time there lived a man who had a maddening passion for baked beans. He loved them, but they always had a very embarrassing and somewhat lively reaction on him. Then one day he met a girl, and fell in love. When it was apparent that they would marry, he thought to himself 'She is such a sweet and gentle girl, she will never go for this kind of carrying on.' So he made the supreme sacrifice and gave up beans. They were married shortly thereafter.

Some months later his car broke down on the way home from work, and since they lived in the country he called his wife and told her that he would be late because he had to walk home. On his way, he passed a small cafe and the odor of freshly baked beans was overwhelming. Since he still had several miles to walk, he figured that he would work off any ill effects before he got home, so he stopped at the cafe. Before leaving, he had eaten three large orders of baked beans. All the way home he putt-putted and after arriving he felt reasonably safe that he had putt-putted his last. His wife seemed somewhat agitated and excited to see him and exclaimed delightedly 'Darling, I have the most wonderful surprise for dinner tonight.' She then blindfolded him and led him to his chair at the head of the dining table. He seated himself and just as she was ready to remove the blindfold, the telephone rang. She made him vow not to touch the blindfold until she returned, then went to answer the phone. Seizing the opportunity he shifted his weight to one leg and let go. It was not only loud, but as ripe as rotten eggs. He took the napkin from his lap and vigorously fanned the air about him. Things had just resumed to normal when he felt another urge coming on him, so he shifted his weight to the other leg and let go again. This was a true prize-winner. While keeping his ear on the conversation in the hall, he went on like this for ten minutes until he knew the phone farewells indicated the end of his freedom. He placed his napkin on his lap and folded his hands on top of it, and smiling contentedly to himself, was the very picture of innocence when his wife returned, apologizing for taking so long. She asked if he had peeked and he, of course, assured her that he had not. At this point she removed the blindfold and there was his surprise.

(fold here)

Twelve dinner guests seated around the table for a 'Happy Birthday Party' for him.

THE W.C.

An English Lady, while visiting Switzerland, was looking for a room, so she asked the schoolmaster if he could recommend any. He took her to see several rooms and, when everything was settled, the lady returned home to make the final preparations to move. When she arrived home, the thought suddenly occurred to her that she had not seen a W.C. around the place. She immediately wrote a note to the schoolmaster asking him if there was a W.C.

The school master was a very poor student of English, so he asked the Parish Priest if he could help him in the matter. Together they tried to discover the meaning of W.C. and came to the conclusion that it meant Wayside Chapel. The school master then wrote the following note to the English Lady:

Dear Madam,

I take great pleasure in informing you that the W.C. is situated nine miles from the house, in the centre of pine groves, surrounded by lovely trees. It is capable of seating 220 people and is open on Sundays and Thursdays only. As there are a great number of people expected during the summer months, I would suggest that you come early, although there is plenty of standing room. This is an unfortunate situation, particularly if you are in the habit of going regularly.

You will no doubt be glad to hear that a good number bring their lunch and make a day of it, while others who can afford to go by car, arrive just in time. I would recommend your Ladyship to go on Thursdays when there is an organ accompaniment, the acoustics are excellent and even the most delicate sound can be heard everywhere. It may interest you to know that my daughter was married in the W.C. and it was there that she first met her husband. I can remember the rush for seats, there were ten people to a seat, usually occupied by one. It was wonderful to see the expressions on their faces.

The newest attraction is a bell donated by a resident of this district. It rings each time a person enters. A bazaar is to be held to provide plush seats for all, since the people feel that it is a long felt need. My wife is rather delicate so she can't attend regularly. It is almost a year since she went last. Naturally it pains her very much not to be able to go more often.

I shall be delighted to reserve the best seat for you if you wish, where you will be seen by all. For the children, there is a special time and place so that they will not disturb the elders.

I remain,

The School Master

An old church decided to repair its properties and employed an artist to touch up an old painting. Upon presenting his bill, the Committee in charge refused payment unless the details were specified, whereupon he presented the articles as follows:

To correcting the Ten Commandments 5.12

Embellishing Pontius Pilate and putting new ribbons on
his hat 3.02

Putting new tail on the Rooster of St. Peter and mending
his comb 2.30

Re-plumbing and gilding left wing of the Guardian Angel 5.18

Washing the servant of the High Priest and putting
Carmine on his cheeks 5.02

Renewing Heaven, adjusting the stars and cleaning the
moon 7.14

Touching up Purgatory and restoring lost souls 3.00

Brightening up the flames of Hell, putting new tail on the
Devil, mending his left hoof and doing several odd jobs
for the damned 7.17

Re-bordering the robes of Herod and adjusting his wig 4.00

Taking spots off the son of Tobias 1.30

Cleaning Balaam's ass and putting one shoe on him 1.70

Putting earrings in Sarah's ears 1.71

Putting new stones in David's sling, enlarging the head of
Goliath and extending Saul's legs 6.13

Decorating Noah's Ark and putting head on Shem 4.31

Mending the shirt of the Prodigal Son and cleaning his ear 3.39

TOTAL £60.49

DOES IT PAY TO ADVERTISE?

A young lady, several months pregnant, boarded a bus and sat opposite a young man. He started smiling at her and, feeling rather embarrassed because of her condition, she moved her seat further along the bus. Again he smiled and again she moved until, after the fourth time of shifting her position, the young man burst out laughing. She told the conductor who stopped the bus, called a policeman and the young man was sent to court.

When the case came up he was asked what he had to say, and he made the following statement:

'When the young lady boarded the bus, I could not help noticing her condition. She first sat under an advertisement which read "COMING SHORTLY – 'THE GOLD DUST TWINS'" and I could not help smiling. She then moved further along under another which read "USE SLOAN'S TO RELIEVE THAT SWELLING" and I was more amused than ever. She then moved for a third time and sat under another advertisement which read "WILLIAM'S STICK DID THE TRICK" and I could hardly control myself. But when she moved again under another which read "DUNLOP RUBBER WOULD HAVE PREVENTED THIS ACCIDENT", well, I had to burst out laughing.'

Case Dismissed

WOMEN'S LIB

A young couple just married were in their honeymoon suite on their wedding night. As they undressed for bed the husband who was a big burly bruiser, tossed his pants to his bride and said, 'Here put these on.' She put them on and the waist was twice the size of her body. 'I can't wear your pants!' she said. 'That's right!' said the husband, 'and don't you forget it. I'm the man who wears the pants in this family!' With that she flipped him her panties and said, 'Try these on.' He tried them on and found he could only get them on as far as his knee cap. He said, 'Hell I can't get into your pants!' She said 'That's right, and that's the way it's going to be until your goddamn attitude changes!'

AIN'T IT THE TRUTH?

It seems that when the great Creator was making the world he called man aside and bestowed upon him 20 years of normal sex life. Man was horrified! Only 20 years! he asked? The Creator didn't budge. That was all he would give him.

Then he called the monkey and gave him 20 years. But I don't need 20 years the monkey protested! Ten years is plenty. Man spoke up and said, 'May I have the other 10 years?' The monkey graciously agreed.

Then the lion was called and given 20 years. The lion too, only needed 10 years. Again man asked, 'May I have the other 10 years?' The lion roared, 'Of course!'

Then came the donkey. He was given 20 years, but like the others, 10 years was enough. So man asked for the spare 10 years and got them.

This explains why man has 20 years of normal sex life, 10 years of monkeying around, 10 years of lion about it, and 10 years of making an ass of himself.

THE CHICKEN

Did you hear about the guy who, when asked by his wife to go to the grocery store, would always stop by for a drink or two and not get home for several hours – without the groceries. Well, this one night, his wife was really mad about him forgetting the frying chicken that she had sent him after; she yelled at him, told him that she wanted a FRESH frying chicken. So he decided, ah ha, he would get a fresh one; went to a poultry farm and picked out a live one!

He started home with the chicken tucked under his arm and, as he was walking by the theatre, realized that the current movie playing was one that he had been wanting to see. So he went up to buy a ticket, the gal at the ticket booth said, 'No way fella, not with a chicken under your arm'. So he decides to go on home; but, as he was walking away, noticed that it was the last night for the showing, so, he goes around the corner, stuffs the chicken down the front of his pants, and goes back and bought a ticket, goes in and sits down by two little old ladies.

Everything went fine until it began to get warm in the theatre and the chicken started moving around because it couldn't breathe very well. The dude reaches down and unzips his fly so that the chicken can stick its head out. The little old lady next to him elbows the gal next to her, 'Mildred, Mildred, this guy next to me has his thing out.'

'So what? If you've seen one, you've seen them all.'

'Not one like this, Mildred, it's eating my popcorn!'

THE 747 HAS EVERYTHING

A man travelling by plane was in urgent need of a toilet, each time he tried the door it was occupied. The stewardess, aware of his predicament, suggested he used the Ladies Room, but cautioned him against pressing the buttons on the wall marked P.P., W.W., W.A. and A.T.R.

Eventually his curiosity got the better of him and sitting there he carefully pressed the first button marked W.W. Immediately warm water sprayed gently under his entire bottom, he thought 'Golly, these girls have it made for them'.

His curiosity not satisfied, he pressed the next button marked W.A., warm air dried his bottom completely, this, he thought, was wonderful. The button marked P.P. when pressed yielded a large powder puff, which patted his bottom with scented talc. Wow, he thought – now for the last button.

Time passed and the next he remembered was lying in hospital, in a panic, he shouted for a nurse, 'What am I doing here? The last thing I remember was being in the Ladies Room aboard a plane'.

The nurse replied, 'So you were, but you were cautioned about the buttons on the wall, you were going great guns until you pressed A.T.R., which stands for Automatic Tampax Remover, so here you are and your penis is under your pillow!!!'

Three men, an architect, a mathematician, and a Government worker got together to brag about their dogs. Each one thought his dog was the smartest and had fantastic abilities. So they decided to show each other what their respective dogs could do.

The architect called to his dog, T-square, gave him a piece of chalk and told him to draw a square, a circle, a triangle, and an isosceles, which the dog did very accurately.

The mathematician agreed that T-square was a very remarkable dog. 'But let me show you what my dog can do.' He called his dog, Slide Rule, and said, 'I'll show you what a really smart dog can do.' He told Slide Rule to go to a pile of cookies and bring him back a dozen, which Slide Rule did without hesitation. 'Now Slide Rule, separate them into equal parts,' and Slide Rule divided the cookies into four stacks of three each.

They all agreed that this was quite a feat.

Then the Government worker said he had watched both dogs do fantastic things. 'But let me show you a **really** clever animal.' He called to his dog and said, 'Now Coffee Break, show them what **you** can do.' Without hesitation, Coffee Break immediately ate all the cookies and went home on sick leave.

A MODERN RED RIDING HOOD
MAKES A POINT

Once upon a time, in a far-away country, there lived a little girl called Red Riding Hood. One day her mother asked her to take a basket of fruit to her grandmother, who had been ill and lived alone in a cottage in the forest.

It happened that a wolf was lurking in the bushes and overheard the conversation. He decided to take a short-cut to the grandmother's house and get the goodies for himself. The wolf killed the grandmother, then dressed in her nightgown and jumped into bed to await the little girl. When she arrived, he made several nasty suggestions and then tried to grab her. But by this time the child was very frightened and ran screaming from the cottage.

A woodcutter, working nearby, heard her cries and rushed to the rescue. He killed the wolf with his axe, thereby saving Red Riding Hood's life. All the townspeople hurried to the scene and proclaimed the woodcutter a hero.

But at the inquest, several facts emerged:
    (1)   The wolf had never been advised of his rights.
    (2)   The woodcutter had made no warning swings before striking the fatal blow.
    (3)   The Civil Liberties Union stressed the point that, although the act of eating Grandma may have been in bad taste, the wolf was only 'doing his thing' and thus didn't deserve the death penalty.
    (4)   The SDS contended that the killing of the grandmother should be considered self-defense since she was over 30 and, therefore, couldn't be taken seriously because the wolf was trying to make love, not war.

On the basis of these considerations, it was decided there was no valid basis for charges against the wolf. Moreover, the woodcutter was indicted for unaggravated assault with a deadly weapon.

Several nights later the woodcutter's cottage was burned to the ground.

One year from the date of 'The Incident at Grandma's,' her cottage was made a shrine for the wolf who had bled and died there. All the village officials spoke about the dedication, but it was Red Riding Hood who gave the most touching tribute.

She said that, while she had been selfishly grateful for the woodcutter's intervention, she realized in retrospect that he had over-reacted. As she knelt and placed a wreath in honor of the brave wolf, there wasn't a dry eye in the whole forest.

VERSE & WORSE

MOTION 23

THATCHER IS MY SHEPHERD

I SHALL NOT WANT

SHE LEADETH ME BESIDE THE STILL FACTORIES

SHE DEPRIVED ME OF OIL

SHE GUIDED ME TO THE PATH OF UNEMPLOYMENT

FOR THE PARTY'S SAKE

I FEAR NO EVIL FOR THOU ART AGAINST ME

SHE ANOINTED MY WAGES WITH PRICE INCREASES SO MY

EXPENSES RUNNETH OVER MY INCOME

SURELY POVERTY AND HARD LIVING SHALL FOLLOW ME

AND I SHALL LIVE IN A MORTGAGED HOUSE FOR EVER

FIVE THOUSAND YEARS AGO MOSES SAID PARK YOUR

CAMEL PICK UP YOUR SHOVEL AND MOUNT YOUR ASS AND

I WILL LEAD YOU TO THE PROMISED LAND

FIVE THOUSAND YEARS LATER ROOSEVELT SAID

LAY DOWN YOUR SHOVEL SIT ON YOUR ASS AND SMOKE

YOUR CAMEL THIS IS THE PROMISED LAND

TODAY THATCHER WILL TAKE YOUR SHOVEL SELL YOUR

CAMEL KICK YOUR ASS AND TELL YOU THERE IS

NO PROMISED LAND

I AM GLAD I AM BRITISH I AM GLAD I AM FREE

BUT I WISH I WERE A DOG AND THATCHER A TREE

A PRAYER FOR OUR TIMES

OUR FATHER WHICH ART IN DOWNING STREET

HAROLD BE THY NAME.

UNITED KINGDOM GONE,

WE SHALL BE DONE ON EARTH, AND PROBABLY IN HEAVEN.

GIVE US EACH DAY OUR DEARER BREAD

AND FORGIVE US OUR DEVALUATIONS,

AS WE FORGIVE THEM THAT SPECULATE AGAINST US.

LEAD US NOT INTO THE COMMON MARKET

BUT DELIVER US FROM THE UNIONS.

FOR THIS IS THE KINGDOM, NO POWER, NO TORY,

FOR EVER AND EVER.

AMIN.

There is something I don't know
    That I am supposed to know.
I don't know <u>what</u> it is I don't know,
    And yet am <u>supposed</u> to know.
And I feel I look stupid
    If I seem both not to know it
    And not know <u>what</u> it is I don't know.
Therefore I pre<u>tend</u> I know it.
    This is nerve-racking
    Since I don't know what I must pretend to know.
Therefore I pretend to know everything.

I feel you know what I am supposed to know.
But you can't tell what it is
Because you don't know that I don't know what it is.

You may know what I don't know, but not
    That I don't know it,
And I can't tell you.
    So you will have to tell me everything.

They gave me a job in the office today,
    With a hole and a couple of grooves:
It's only a cleat to go under a door
    To restrain it whenever it moves.
To sketch it would take but a couple of lines,
    Plus a working dimension or two,
But these wouldn't show nearly how much I know,
    So I'm sure that they never would do.
I'll cut it all up into sections,
    With a symbol beside every part.
I want to be sure that I make it obscure
    As to where the machining will start.
It's time to put on the dimensions and then,
    That's the spot where I really unload:
I'll mark all the lines with mysterious signs,
    That an Einstein could never decode.
My drawing is finished and printed at last,
    And I'm proud of its hazy design.
I know they'll have ulcers and chaos and such,
    When at last it comes out on the line.
A feeling of pride starts a stirring inside
    As my tracing is filed on the shelf:
My quest has been solved with a print so involved
    That I can't even read it myself.

I'M FINE, THANK YOU.

There is nothing the matter with me,
I'm as healthy as I can be,
I have arthritis in both my knees,
And when I talk, I talk with a wheeze.
My pulse is weak and my blood is thin
But I'm awfully well for the shape I'm in.

    Arch supports I have for my feet
    Or I wouldn't be able to be on the street.
    Sleep is denied me night after night,
    But every morning I find I'm all right.
    My memory is failing, my head's in a spin
    But I'm awfully well for the shape I am in.

The moral is this as my tale I'll unfold,
That for you and me who are growing old,
It's better to say: 'I am fine' with a grin,
Than to let folks know the shape we are in.

    How do I know that my youth is all spent?
    Well, my get up and go has got up and went.
    But I really don't mind when I think with a grin
    Of all the grand places my get up has been.

Old age is golden I have oft heard it said,
But sometimes I wonder as I get into bed,
With my ears in the drawer, my teeth in a cup,
My eyes on the table until I wake up,
Ere sleep overtakes me I say to myself,
'Is there anything else I could lay on the shelf?'

    When I was young my slippers were red,
    I could kick my heels right over my head.
    When I was older my slippers were blue,
    But still I could dance the whole night through.
    Now I am old, my slippers are black,
    I walk to the store and puff my way back.

I get up each morning and dust off my wits,
I pick up the paper and read the obits,
If my name is still missing, I know I'm not dead
So I have a good breakfast and go back to bed.

The sky so blue
The moon so bright
we're alone just you and I

Her hair so black
her eyes so bright
I knew just what she
wanted to night.

So with my courage
I tried my best
I layed my fingers upon
her breast
Her shape so round
her looks so fine
Fran my fingers down
her spine
I trembled with her
beating heart as she
slowly spread her
legs apart
So if your thinking
bad things right now.
It was only my first
experience milking a cow

MAGGIE HALL

This is the tale of Maggie Hall
Who had no money left at all
One night when going to the flickers
She found she hadn't any knickers.

This put poor Maggie in a stew
She didn't know just what to do
And as the night was rather chilly
To go without them would be silly.

She looked at all the pairs she'd got
And found they'd all begun to rot
With every pair in bad condition
A hole in quite the wrong position.

She thought she'd better make a pair
So started searching everywhere
She found a piece of boracic lint
With quite a lovely pinkish tint.

Thought Maggie "this will be alright
To make a pair just for tonight,
In the dark they'll look like satin."
So set to work with paper pattern.

She made the legs both long and wide
And put the fluffy part inside
In half an hour or thereabouts
She'd made a smashing pair of clouts.

She put them on and left her home
To meet the boyfriend from the 'drome
And so they sat and watched the flicks
With Mag in medicated knicks.

But late that night with weary head
As Mag undressed to go to bed
She cried "my goodness, what disgrace
It's healed it up without a trace."

The moral here is plain to see
And you can take a tip from me
If you can't buy them from the stores
Don't use boracic lint for drawers.

THE NIGHT BEFORE CHRISTMAS

'Twas the night before Christmas and all thru the house
Were empties and butts left around by some louse.
And the best quart I hid in the chimney with care
Had been swiped by some bum who'd found it down there.

My guests had long since been poured in their beds
To wake in the morning with some gosh-awful heads.
My wife too was cold with her chin in her lap
And me, I was dying for one more nightcap.

When out from my lawn there arose such a tissy
I sprang from my bed — oh, was I dizzy!
Away to the window I tore like a flash,
Fell over the table, broke a chair with a crash.

The moon on the breast of the new fallen snow
Made me think of the coal bill and all I did owe.
When what to my wondering eyes did show up
But eight bloated reindeer hitched to a beer truck.

With a little old driver who looked like a hick
But I saw it was Santa as tight as a tick.
Like General Grant tanks those reindeer they came
And he hiccoughed and belched as he called them by name.

'On Schenley, on Seagram, we ain't got all night
You too, Haig and Haig, and you, Black and White.
Scram up on the roof, get off this wall,
Get going you dummies, we got a long haul.'

So up on the roof went reindeer and truck
But a tree branch hit Santa before he could duck.
And then in a twinkle I heard from above
A heck of a noise that was no cooing dove.

Then I pulled in my head and cocked a sharp ear.
Down the chimney he came right smack on his rear.
He was dressed in furs and had cuffs on his pants
And the way the guy squirmed, I guess he had ants.

His droll little mouth made him look a bit wacky
And the beard on his chin was stained with tobaccy.
He had pints and quarts in the sack on his back
And a breath that would blow a train off the track.

He was chubby and plump and he tried to stand right
But he didn't fool me, he was high as a kite.
He spoke not a word but went straight to work
And missed half the stockings, the plastered old jerk.

Then putting five fingers to the end of his nose
He gave one the bird and up the chimney he rose.
He sprang to his truck and slid on his face
He finally managed to flip flop into place.

And I heard him burp 'ere he passed out of sight,
'MERRY CHRISTMAS, YOU RUM-DUMS, NOW REALLY GET
   TIGHT!'

Remember when HIPPIE meant big in the hips
and a TRIP involved travel in cars, planes and ships?
When a POT was a vessel for cooking things in,
and HOOKED was what Grandma's rugs might have been?

When FIX was a verb that meant to repair,
and to be IN meant simply existing somewhere?
When NEAT meant organized, tidy and clean,
and GRASS was ground cover, normally green?

When SWITCHES, not people, were turned on and off,
and the PILL was something we took for a cough?
When FUZZ was a substance that was fluffy like lint,
and BREAD came from bakeries, not from the mint?

When GROOVY meant furrowed with channels and hollows,
and BIRDS were winged creatures, like robins and swallows?
When ROLL meant a bun, and ROCK was a stone,
and HANG-UP was something you did to a phone?

When CHICKEN was poultry, and BAG was a sack,
and JUNK was trash, cast-offs and old bric-a-brac?
When JAM was preserves, that you spread on your bread,
and CRAZY meant barmy, not right in the head?

When CAT was a feline, a kitten grown up,
and TEA was a liquid you drank from a cup?
When SWINGER was someone who swung in a swing,
and a PAD was a soft, sort of cushiony thing?

When WAY OUT meant distant and far, far away,
and a man couldn't sue you for calling him GAY,
When DIG meant to shovel and spade in the dirt,
and PUT ON was what you did with a shirt?

When SQUARE was a 90-degree, four angled form,
and COOL was a temperature lower than warm?
When CAMP meant to quarter outdoors in a tent,
and POP was what the weasel went?

When TOUGH described meat too unyielding to chew,
and MAKING A SCENE was a rude thing to do?
If you can recall, be you Jack or Jill,
You're over the hill, friend you're over the hill!!

Words once so sensible, sober and serious,
are making the FREAK SCENE like PSYCHE DELIRIOUS.
It's GROOVY, Man, GROOVY, but English, it's not,
Me thinks that the language has gone straight to POT!

. . . Author unknown.

FLOOD LINES

And the Lord said unto Noah: 'Where is the ark which I have commanded thee to build?'

And Noah said unto the Lord: 'Verily I have had three carpenters off ill. The gopher wood supplier hath let me down – yea, even though the gopher wood hath been on order for nigh upon twelve months.'

And God said unto Noah: 'I want that ark finished even after seven days and seven nights.'

And Noah said: 'It will be so.'
And it was not so.

And the Lord said: 'What seemeth to be the trouble this time?'

And Noah said unto the Lord: 'Mine subcontractor hath gone bankrupt. The pitch which Thou commandeth me to put on the outside and on the inside of the ark hath not arrived. The plumber hath gone on strike. Shem, my son, who helpeth me on the ark side of the business, hath formed a pop group with his brother Ham and Japheth. Lord, I am undone.'

And the Lord grew angry and said: 'And what about the unicorns and the fowls of the air by sevens?'

And Noah wrung his hands and wept saying: 'Lord, unicorns are a discontinued line; thou canst not get them for love nor money. And it hath just been told me that the fowls of the air are sold only in half dozens. Lord, Lord, Thou knoweth how it is.'

And the Lord in his wisdom said: 'Noah, my son, I know. Why else dost thou think that I will cause a flood to descend upon the earth?'

A SECRETARY'S PRAYER

Give me please, O Lord, the wisdom of a Judge, the patience of Job, and the hide of an elephant.

Give my fingers such speed that I can finish tonight the mail I should have been given yesterday. Give me such acute hearing that I can understand the dictation he mumbles out of the window while jingling the change in his pocket.

Give me that mental ability which will enable me to remind him of appointments he forgot to mention, and give me the diplomacy of an ambassador to get seats for trains, planes and theatres which he was so sure he had told me about yesterday.

Give me please a magic box out of which I can instantly produce the envelopes, pens, pencils, letters, files, lighter flints, funny notes and buttons he has lost.

Help me to correct his spelling and even worse phrasing so that he reads my letters and glows with pride at his own good English – and let me suffer no pangs if he scrawls alterations in ink which I could so easily have dubbed in quite neatly on my machine.

Caution me to remember that if one day he feels off colour and barks, snarls or sneers, I must retain a gentle, friendly smile no matter how well or ill I may happen to feel.

Give me an uncanny insight and an encyclopaedic memory for dates and anniversaries he has never even mentioned and meetings he forgets to record.

Help me to have a memory three years long. By some small miracle let me be able to do all things at once – answer three telephones at the same time and type a letter that 'must go today' even though I know it won't get signed until tomorrow.

Give me the knowledge of a university professor with my junior certificate of education. Help me to understand and carry out all intructions without any explanation.

Let me know, without being told, where my boss is or when he'll get back. When he happens to disappear without a trace just when something desperately urgent crops us, please give me the qualities of Sherlock Holmes so that I may track him down.

Could you then please, O Lord, extend your mercies and throw in just one extra lesson on how to combine the duties of Secretary, Chairwoman, Hostess, Diplomat, Accountant, Receptionist, Filing Clerk, Booking Clerk, Cloakroom Attendant and General Nurse.

LORD, IF YOU COULD, I WOULD BE SINCERELY GRATEFUL